Medical Marijuana Law

Richard Glen Boire, Esq.
& Kevin Feeney, Esq.

RONIN

Berkeley, Cailfornia

Medical Marijuana Law

Copyright 2006 by Richard Glen Boire & Kevin Feeney
ISBN: 1-57951-034-5; 978-1-57951-034-3
E-ISBN: 1-57951-078-7; 978-1-57951-078-7

Published by
Ronin Publishing, Inc.
PO Box 22900
Oakland, CA 94609
www.roninpub.com

Production:
Editor: Beverly A. Potter (docpotter.com)
Cover Design: Brian Groppe (briangroppe.com)
Book Design: Beverly A. Potter

Fonts:
Baskerville: Monotype, Agfa
Venis: Chank

Library of Congress Card Number: 2006938948
Distributed to the book trade by **Publishers Group West**
Printed in the United States by **Delta Printing Solutions**

Medical
Marijuana Law

We greatly appreciate Bruce Mirken, Director of Communication at the Marijuana Policy Project (MPP) for his support and the generosity of MPP in contributing their Model State Medical Marijuana law to this Work. We also appreciate Dr. Frank Lucido for his helpful comments on the chapter discussing physicans' responsibilities and his pithy comments in the Preface regarding the need for high standards of care for medical marijuana patients; and Dale Gieringer, State Coordinator of California NORML for his excellent advice to marijuana providers. And we especially appreciate the unsung heros who helped birth this Work. Thanks!

Table of Contents

Also by Richard Glen Boire:

Marijuana Law

Sacred Mushrooms & the Law

Journal of Cognitive Liberties (Editor)

Entheogen Law Reporter (Editor)

Salvia Divinorum Growers Guide (Translator)

Preface

by Frank Lucido, M.D.

Boire and Feeney's new book *Medical Marijuana Law* has been published at a critical time for the movement to recognize cannabis as a legitimate medical treatment. In California, we have recently experienced a proliferation of "quick in, quick out" clinics that have sprung up next to dispensaries, offering brief evaluations, with minimal documentation of patients diagnoses or previous treatments and poor follow-up of the patients illness or symptoms. In an effort to solve this problem, I and others have been working to raise the quality of the medical cannabis consultation by maintaining standards of care for medical cannabis patients that are comparable to those that pertain to any other aspect of patient care.

The two most frequently cited reasons that physicians give for not employing this safe and effective medicine in patient care are concerns about their own legal status and lack of training in the clinical use of cannabis as a medicine. The clinical judgment and expertise that a physician uses in encounters with cannabis patients does not differ significantly from that needed to care for patients with similar conditions who choose conventional treatments. If a patient is receiving ongoing adequate and appropriate care for a serious illness, documentation should be easily obtainable from the treating provider. Still, patients considering the use of cannabis as a medicine do pose some specific challenges to the recommending physician.

Quality Standards Needed

The medical cannabis consultation provided to both health care provider-referred and self-referred patients according to my standard of care is specifically for the management of symptoms of a previously diagnosed and treated serious illness. Seriously ill patients who obtains symptom relief from the use of medical cannabis, particularly those who plan to grow their own medicine, need a credible recommendation. Even patients who are already aware that cannabis provides relief for their symptoms and who have worked out the amount and method of cannabis use that works best for them continue to need an accessible, knowledgeable, trustworthy physician who maintains good documentation, applies customary standards of clinical knowledge, and who is prepared to explain the decision to recommend cannabis in a court of law if necessary. In some ways, this is the primary contribution that a cannabis recommending physician makes to the medico-legal well being of cannabis knowledgeable patients who have otherwise adequate care for their serious illness.

Unfortunately, some of the abuses that characterize the attempts of poor-quality HMO's to limit the time and attention paid to patients in the interests of economy have been surfacing in the care of medical cannabis patients as well. Clinics that provide patients with a 3 to 15 minute encounter with a physician or physician extender, that require no documentation of diagnosis, that produce very abbreviated medical documentation, and that may or may not be available to verify a patient's recommendation for law enforcement should the need arise, have sprung up in California. Some of these are closely allied to cannabis dispensaries, perform cross referrals to specific dispensaries or are located in or adjacent to dispensaries. I would compare the usefulness of a recommendation from these clinics to a "fig leaf"—it gives the appearance of propriety, but doesn't really cover anything.

These clinics and providers are putting the medical cannabis law at risk. The courts have traditionally been skeptical of allowing the habits of the majority of physicians to determine what is appropriate care. Supreme Court Justice Oliver Wendell Holmes, for example, wrote that "What is usually done may be evidence of what ought to be done, but what ought to be done is set by the standards of reasonable prudence, whether it is complied with or not." (*Texas and Pacific Railroad v. Behymer*, 189 U.S. 468, 470 (1903).

Fig leaf-type recommendations put the medical cannabis law at risk.

Patients whose physicians fail to adhere to accepted standards of medical responsibility in the care of their medical cannabis patients undermine the credibility of the entire medical cannabis movement by providing opportunities for fraud and abuse, and provoking public opinion backlash. We have seen this take the form of restrictive zoning, moratoria on the opening of medical cannabis dispensaries, "sting" operations using fake patients to entrap doctors and clinics and sensationalized and inaccurate news stories that defame both cannabis patients and providers.

A physician recommendation is only as valuable as its credibility and protective value as determined by a judge and jury after the doctor, the patient, and

any expert witnesses have been questioned. This can
be an expensive proposition for the patient. A better
outcome would be to prevent the patient having to
go to court at all. Some patients and their physicians
may plan to do what patients have been doing from
the 1940's through the passage of the California
Compassionate Use Act in 1996 ("Prop 215"): Not get
caught. Patients who do not think that they will ever
be asked to prove that they have a recommendation,
or a physician who thinks their recommendations will
never be challenged in a court of law may feel that
"economizing" by using "fig leaf" minimal standards of
evaluation and documentation for cannabis patients
may be acceptable.

If we hope to employ cannabis as an unexceptional
therapy free of inappropriate legal constraint, medical
cannabis decision making should conform to the
usual and customary standards of quality care in the
community Physicians who fail to educate themselves
about medical cannabis law, who tolerate or even
encourage abbreviated assembly-line care, who cross-
refer to cannabis dispensaries, who encourage routine
walk-in clients, who do not require documentation of
the patient's diagnosis and the ongoing care of their
serious illnesses put the legitimacy of the medical
cannabis law at risk.

Even high standards of medical ethics and
professionalism may not protect either patients or
clinicians against overzealous law enforcement. But
cannabis-recommending physicians who understand the
medical cannabis laws that apply in their communities,
who adhere to the limits set out in the Conant decision
of the Ninth Circuit and avoid "aiding and abetting," and
who do not refer to cannabis dispensaries should sleep
better knowing they are doing all they can to protect
their patients and themselves. An ongoing effort to be
legally as well as medically knowledgeable promotes

better patient care and patient safety. Physicians who
are not available to verify patients' recommendations
when contacted by law enforcement, or are not able
and willing to testify competently in support of
their patients' medical cannabis use jeopardize their
patient's legal safety and may expose their patients to
considerable legal fees.

It is my hope that more community-based clinicians
in both primary care and specialty practice will begin
to make cannabis recommendations—while adhering
to quality standards expected from a physician. By
following these guidelines and by a diligent effort to
understand and adhere to the laws relating to the use
of cannabis as medicine, it is possible to protect both
seriously ill patients and responsible medical cannabis
clinicians. Boire and Feeney's *Medical Marijuana Law*
provides a new and valuable resource for achieving this
goal.

—Frank H. Lucido M.D.
Berkeley, California

Dr. Frank Lucido is a leading expert on the clinical use of
medical cannabis and on protecting the rights of legitimate
patients who use cannabis medicinally and responsible
physicians who recommend it. He is widely known to be
a thorough, caring, and trusted physician, who takes the
time to establish that patients are appropriate in their use
of medical cannabis, as well as having defensible medical
records demonstrating it.

For Dr. Lucido's survey of California cannabis recommending
physicians, see www.medboardwatch.com/survey.htm.
Patients who have questions about cannabis dispensaries
can obtain this information from California NORML's website
(www.canorml.org). Physicians who wish to review Dr.
Lucido's standards for medical cannabis practice can find
them at MedicalBoardWatch (www.medboardwatch.com/
implementation-of-7-year-plan.htm).

History of Medical Marijuana Use

A glimpse into the history of medicinal marijuana use helps to understand the current debate over medicinal marijuana use. Of course, this chapter is not a comprehensive study of marijuana's history. There are many great resources that explore the history of marijuana, its medical and other uses, as well as the history of marijuana prohibition. See the bibliography for some of our favorite sources.

The use of marijuana for medicinal purposes is nothing new. Marijuana has been used for millennia in the treatment of various medical conditions, with the earliest accounts of its medical uses in China, India, and the Middle East. Later, marijuana became an accepted medical remedy in the West, and found its way to the shelves of U.S. pharmacies by the mid-19th Century.

China

The earliest recorded occurrence of marijuana's use as a medicine dates back at least to the third millennium, B.C., when the plant's medicinal powers were investigated by the Legendary Chinese Emperor Shen Nung, who is popularly known as the

"Father of Chinese Medicine." In the *Pen Ts'ao Ching*, an ancient Chinese pharmacopoeia thought to collect the works of Shen Nung, an elixir of hemp is recommended for the treatment of malaria and rheumatic pains, among other ailments. Marijuana was later used by Hua Tuo, a famous 2nd Century A.D. physician, as an analgesic and an anesthetic. By the time of European contact, Chinese use of marijuana as a medicine had declined.

India

In India, marijuana is used in Ayurvedic medicine. Marijuana is listed as an ingredient in numerous preparations in the *Anandakanda*, a 10th Century Indian Medical treatise, which is still used by some Ayurvedic doctors today. Marijuana, which is called either *vijaya* or *bhanga*, was used to treat diarrhea, diabetes, tuberculosis, asthma, elephantiasis, anemia and rabies, among other ailments.

The Middle East

The medical use of marijuana in the Middle East is first mentioned in a 7th Century B.C. religious text known as the *Venidad*, a volume of the *Zend-Avesta*, thought to have been written by Zoroaster. Later, during the reign of the Roman Empire, marijuana was used as an analgesic and anesthetic, and used to treat migraines, syphilis and other medical problems.

Europe

In Europe, the use of marijuana as a medicine was recommended in several prominent medical texts, the most notable of which is Dioscoride's *Materia Medica*, which is dated to 65 A.D., but was considered a fundamental medical text well into the 17th Century.

It would be centuries until marijuana was next mentioned in William Turner's *New Herbal*, published in 1538, where it was promoted as a therapeutic agent. Marijuana was praised as a medicine in a book by John Gerard in 1597, and was recommended to treat depression in *The Anatomy of Melancholy*, written by Robert Burton in 1621. *The Complete Herbal*, published in 1649 by Nicholas Culpeper, recommended marijuana in the treatment of coughs, jaundice, joint pain, inflammation and indigestion among other ailments.

In the 19th Century, marijuana emerged as a mainstream medicine in the West. Studies in the 1840s by a French doctor by the name of Jacques-Joseph Moreau found that marijuana suppressed headaches, increased appetites, and aided people to sleep. William Brooke O'Shaugnessy, an Irish doctor, studied the effects of hashish on canines in the 1830s and presented his findings that hashish was a valuable anti-convulsive remedy to the Medical and Physical Society of Bengal in 1839. Then, in 1842, a London Pharmacist named Peter Squire made the first known tincture of cannabis, using hashish that had been provided by O'Shaugnessy. This tincture, essentially an extract of hashish in alcohol, would later be legally sold in the U.S. as "Tilden's Extract."

It is rumored that Sir Reynolds treated Queen Victoria's menstrual cramps, and related pains, with a preparation of marijuana.

In the late 19th Century, the respected British medical journal *The Lancet* featured an article outlining the use of marijuana to treat the symptoms of opiate withdrawal, and another article by Sir John Russell Reynolds, doctor to Queen Victoria, which described the use of marijuana in treating uterine bleeding, migraines, neuralgia, and epileptic spasms. It is rumored that Sir Reynolds treated Queen Victoria's menstrual cramps, and related pains, with a preparation of marijuana.

United States

By 1850, marijuana had made its way into the United States Pharmacopoeia, which listed marijuana as a treatment for numerous afflictions, including: neuralgia, tetanus, typhus, cholera, rabies, dysentery, alcoholism, opiate addiction, anthrax, leprosy, incontinence, gout, convulsive disorders, tonsillitis, insanity, excessive menstrual bleeding and uterine bleeding, among others. Patented marijuana tinctures were sold by Parke Davis, Eli Lilly, and E. R. Squibb & Sons.

These tinctures, however, had a number of drawbacks. First, it was impossible to judge an appropriate dose. Potency varied from bottle to bottle due to differences in plant potencies and difficulties in processing. Adding to the difficulties was the fact that tinctures would separate out, and if not shaken, the final drop in the bottle could cause an intense hallucinatory experience in the unsuspecting user. Doctors became wary of such "overdoses" because similar experiences with opium could be lethal. In part, because of these difficulties in measurement and dosing, marijuana lost out to opium as the painkiller of choice.

The second drawback to the modern use of marijuana as a medicine was the increasing romanticism surrounding synthetic drugs, and the invention of the syringe in the 1850s. With the technology for creating and processing synthetic drugs, use of herbal products fell by the wayside due to the enthusiasm for new technologies, even though the synthetics were often more harmful than the herbal remedies they replaced.

The advent of the syringe allowed drugs to take effect immediately through injection. Marijuana's active components, however, are not water-soluble and thus cannot be injected. Marijuana can only be taken orally, usually as a tincture, which requires patients to wait at least an hour before any effect would occur. This is regarded as a major drawback favoring opium instead.

Nevertheless, marijuana continued to be used as a popular medicine, with twenty-eight pharmaceutical preparations still in use at the time the Marihuana Tax Act was passed in 1937.

Medical Marijuana Prohibition

Prohibition came unexpectedly for the medical community. Many doctors and pharmacists did not know that the new social menace "marihuana," used predominantly by "Negroes," Mexicans, and Jazz musicians, was the same as *cannabis*, the name used by doctors. The term "marihuana" was of relatively recent usage, having been appropriated by prohibitionists from Mexican communities familiar with the plant's psychoactive properties. The appropriated term assisted the eventual passage of the Marihuana Tax Act by obscured the identity of the plant to be prohibited, by associating marijuana with "undesirable" elements of society, i.e., non-white persons.

The Marihuana Tax Act

The Marihuana Tax Act, which passed in 1937, required all manufacturers, importers, dealers and medical practitioners dealing with marijuana to register with the federal government and to pay a special occupational tax. Transfers to other registrants were to be taxed at a dollar per ounce, whereas transfers to the end user were taxed at the prohibitive amount of *one-hundred* dollars per ounce. While the Act purported to be a Tax Act, the actual effect was the de facto prohibition on all uses of marijuana, including medicinal uses.

Dr. William C. Woodward, a representative of the American Medical Association (AMA) who had previously testified against the bill before the Ways & Means Committee, submitted the following testimony prior to the Act's passage:

> *The obvious purpose and effect of this bill is to impose so many restrictions on the medicinal use as to prevent such use altogether... it may serve to deprive the public of the benefits of a drug that on further research may prove to be of substantial value* (Conrad, 1997, p. 25).

Despite Dr. Woodward's vehement opposition to the Tax Act, the bill passed out of Committee and went to the full Congress for a vote. The debate on the floor of Congress lasted mere minutes, with the only question coming from a Republican congressman who inquired as to the AMA's position on the bill. Democratic congressman Fred M. Vinson responded by lying.

In reference to Dr. Woodward and his testimony Vinson claimed that "Dr. Wharton came down here. They support this bill one hundred percent" (*Bonnie & Whitebread*, 1999, p. 174). Not only did the Congressman perjure himself, but he got Dr. Woodward's name wrong. No one inquired further, and the bill was passed without fanfare or public attention. The Marihuana Tax Act was signed by President Roosevelt on August 2nd, and swiftly took effect on the first of October, 1937.

At the request of Harry Anslinger, head of the Federal Bureau of Narcotics (FBN) and one of the chief architects of the Marihuana Tax Act, marijuana was removed from the United States Pharmacopoeia in 1941.

Marijuana received little attention after that, although the growth of hemp, for cording and canvas, was briefly encouraged to support the war effort.

The Boggs Act

Following World War II, a perceived increase in the use of narcotics along with a growing culture of paranoia, fueled by McCarthyism, led to a new drug hysteria and a new federal law known as "the Boggs Act." The passage of the Boggs Act in 1951 introduced the first round of mandatory minimum sentences for drug crimes. While the Boggs Act focused predominantly on the use of narcotics, the debate leading to its passage cemented the notion that use of marijuana leads to the use of harder drugs, despite significant pharmacological differences from opiates. As a result, for the first time marijuana was lumped together with the traditional narcotics giving birth to the "gateway theory," which continues to influence marijuana prohibition policy today.

Narcotic Control Act

Penalties for marijuana were again increased in 1956 with the passage of the Narcotic Control Act. By the mid-1960s marijuana use had become prevalent among white middle-class youth, and controversy began to surface over whether possession should remain a criminal offense. At the same time, many new substances that had not previously been controlled, such as LSD and psilocybin, emerged and Congress rushed to regulate these substances with the passage of the Drug Abuse Control Amendments of 1965.

The Controlled Substances Act

The Controlled Substances Act (CSA) was passed in 1970 as part of a larger bill, known as the Comprehensive Drug Abuse Prevention and Control

Act, in 1970. The CSA is known for its categorical breakdown of drugs into five Schedules. Drugs are classified into one of these five Schedules based on their abuse potential, harmfulness, and accepted medical value in the US. Schedule I contains the substances said to have the highest potential for abuse, no accepted medical value, and which are considered unsafe even for use under medical supervision.

How to classify marijuana was a bone of contention in Congress. The CSA required the Bureau of Narcotics & Dangerous Drugs (BNDD), which later became the Drug Enforcement Administration (DEA), to base all future scheduling of drugs on sound scientific evidence. Congress, however, was not bound by the procedures it would impose on the BNDD. Congress was prepared to place marijuana into Schedule I without reviewing the scientific evidence, but several congressmen had strong objections, including Senator Ted Kennedy who expressed doubt that current scientific evidence would support a finding that marijuana lacked any medical value. A compromise was struck to temporarily place marijuana in Schedule I, pending the outcome and recommendations of a federal investigation to be undertaken by a Presidential Commission.

The Shafer Commission

The Commission was made up of thirteen members, nine appointed by President Nixon and four by Congress, and given one year to study marijuana and report back its findings. Nixon hand-picked hardliners for the Commission, including former Pennsylvania Governor Raymond Shafer, with the intent of quashing any efforts to reschedule marijuana. Nixon was immediately criticized by reformers for "stacking the deck," but ultimately the cards would not play out in Nixon's favor.

In 1972, the Commission issued its findings in a
report titled *Marihuana: A Signal of Misunderstanding*.
While the Commission unanimously rejected the idea
of legalizing marijuana, they urged the withdrawal of
criminal sanctions for personal use of marijuana. The
Commission also noted that marijuana may prove useful
in "the treatment of glaucoma, migraine, alcoholism
and terminal cancer" (*Randall & O'Leary*, 1998, p. 33).

President Nixon, however, rejected the
recommendations, and decriminalization bills based
on the Commission's recommendation and introduced
in the Senate and the House, languished without
attention. Marijuana use, strongly associated with
the counterculture and the anti-war movements, had
become so politicized that scientific evidence no longer
played much of a role in the debate.

Federal Compassion

Back in 1975, a glaucoma patient by the name of
Robert Randall was busted for possession of four
marijuana plants. While the bust was a fairly routine
operation, the events of that day would eventually
change the course of the marijuana debate. Robert
Randall had discovered quite by accident that marijuana
relieved the symptoms of his glaucoma, an eye disease
that can lead to blindness. He had started growing
marijuana to treat his medical condition.

In the months leading up to his trial, Randall went to
great lengths to gather evidence showing the medical
efficacy of marijuana in the treatment of glaucoma. He
worked with several doctors, participated in research
programs, and investigated the possibility of acquiring
marijuana from the federal government, which it
produced for research purposes. Randall argued at trial
that if he did not use marijuana he would go blind, and
that his use of marijuana was therefore a necessity.

The judge found his argument persuasive, stating:

> *Penalizing one who acted rationally to avoid a greater
> harm will serve neither to rehabilitate the offender nor
> deter others from acting similarly when presented with
> similar circumstances* (Randall & O'Leary, 1998, p. 33).

The judge found Randall *not guilty* due to his "medical
necessity" defense. The medical necessity defense is
discussed in Chapter 5.

In 1976, Randall became the first U.S. citizen
approved to receive federal supplies of marijuana
as part of the government's new "Compassionate"
Investigational New Drug (IND) program. The IND
program allows patients to receive non-FDA approved
drugs on an investigational basis. The program provided
a loophole to the Congressional declaration, contained
in the Controlled Substances Act, that marijuana has no
accepted medical value, and is considered unsafe even
for use under medical supervision.

Yet, even at its height in 1992, only fifteen patients
received federal marijuana under the Compassionate
IND program. By that time, interest in the program
had skyrocketed, largely due to the exploding AIDS
epidemic and the increasing recognition that marijuana
was effective in combating AIDS related wasting-
syndrome and nausea.

That same year, with thirty-two new applications
approved, and another two thousand pending, the
first Bush Administration shut down the program.
The fifteen patients receiving marijuana at that time
were allowed to continue in the program, with final
termination of the program to occur with the rather
morbid sunset provision resting on the death of the
final patient. As of Fall of 2006, seven of the fifteen
patients remained in the program.

New Mexico Challenge

When Randall was the nation's only legal pot-smoker, he became the focus of national attention, and helped thrust the therapeutic value of marijuana into the national spotlight. Following in his footsteps, Lynn Pierson, a young man fighting testicular cancer, took center stage in New Mexico to lobby for medical access to marijuana. Many legislators were convinced that marijuana should be available for sick people like Mr. Pierson, but because of the general prohibition on marijuana, they were unable to devise a system for obtaining and supplying marijuana to patients. As we will discuss later, federal law trumps state law.

Federal law trumps state law

As a result, New Mexico could not grow and supply marijuana without a federal license, which was not likely to be granted. The state considered distributing confiscated marijuana to medical patients, but the federal government was touting the use of the toxic pesticide paraquat to destroy illicit marijuana crops abroad, and the chance that the state would be distributing contaminated marijuana to sick patients was unacceptable. Finally, the New Mexico legislature found a solution. They would create a statewide research program and apply for federal supplies of marijuana.

In 1978, New Mexico became the first state to pass a therapeutic marijuana research program, and to begin receiving marijuana from the federal government. As more states followed New Mexico's lead—eventually a total of 35, the federal government became concerned and devised a strategy for stalling the movement. The federal government defused demand for medical marijuana by pulling a bait-and-switch with synthetic THC.

The plan was first made apparent in 1980, when the state of California requested one million marijuana cigarettes for their program and was forced to take synthetic THC in its place. California was required to revise its program, and received marijuana only for the most seriously ill patients suffering from cancer. During the five years that California's program remained active, only 100 patients actually received marijuana, while almost 2,500 other patients received synthetic THC.

Rescheduling Effort

With the swelling state support for and interest in medical marijuana, congressional representatives in Washington D.C. took notice. In 1981 a bill that would reclassify marijuana as Schedule II, and would establish a system of supply and distribution was introduced as House Resolution 4498 in the 97th Congress. Introduced by four Republicans, the bill was primarily sponsored by Rep. Stewart McKinney (CT) and Newt Gingrich (GA). The list of cosponsors grew to 100 by the beginning of 1982, and was reintroduced in the 98th (1983) and 99th (1985) Congress with similar support, but never received the necessary hearings for a floor vote.

In May 1985, *dronabinol*, a synthetic version of THC, the primary active principle of marijuana, was approved by the FDA, dealing a significant blow to the political support for medical marijuana. Most of the state research programs that had opened in the late 1970s and early 1980s closed by 1988.

All was not bleak, however. Back in 1972, the National Organization for the Reform of Marijuana Laws (NORML) had filed a petition seeking to have marijuana removed from Schedule I. After over a decade of legal wrangling, hearings finally began in 1984. After two years of hearings, on September 6, 1988, Francis L.

Young, the Chief Administrative Law Judge for the DEA, ruled in favor of NORML, declaring:

> *Based upon the facts established in this record ...*
> *one must reasonably conclude that there is accepted*
> *safety for use of marijuana under medical supervision.*
> *To conclude otherwise, on this record, would be*
> *unreasonable, arbitrary and capricious* (DEA, 1988).

Marijuana, said Judge Young, belonged in Schedule II, not Schedule I.

Unfortunately, federal agencies are not bound by the recommendations of their own administrative law judges, and the recommendation—just like the earlier one made by Nixon's Presidential Commission—was rejected on Dec. 29, 1989, by DEA Administrator John Lawn. To this date, marijuana remains in Schedule I, with no exception for medical use under federal law.

The People Take the Initiative

The swell of support for medical marijuana that arose in the 1980s amongst legislators, administrators, and government officials had subsided by the beginning of the 1990s. The great lobbying efforts made by patients and activists had failed, and it had become apparent that the appropriate support would not be found among state or federal legislators. The people needed a way for popular opinion and common sympathy to prevail over the cold and stagnant workings of government, politics and bureaucracy. Fortunately, some parts of the country allow citizens to legislate by popular vote through the initiative process.

San Francisco

The first medical marijuana initiative appeared in the city of San Francisco as Proposition P, which passed with an overwhelming 79% of the vote on Nov.

5, 1991. Proposition P called on the State of California and the California Medical Association to "restore hemp medical preparations to the list of available medicines in California," and not to penalize physicians "from prescribing hemp preparations for medical purposes." Less than a year later, the San Francisco Board of Supervisors passed a resolution urging the local Police Commission and the District Attorney "to make lowest priority the arrest or prosecution of those involved in the possession or cultivation of hemp for medicinal purposes." The resolution also urged the Mayor of San Francisco and the District Attorney "to allow a letter from a treating physician to be used as prima facie evidence that marijuana can alleviate the pain and suffering of that patient's medical condition" (*S. F. Board of Supervisors*, 1992).

Santa Cruz

The next initiative appeared the following year in the city of Santa Cruz as Proposition A, which passed with 77.5% of the vote on Nov. 2, 1992.

Buyers Clubs Emerge

A group known as "AIDS Coalition to Unleash Power," or ACT-UP, had been operating "buyers' clubs," where AIDS patients could purchase AIDS drugs for reduced prices. When the federal government shutdown the Compassionate IND program, these clubs took it upon themselves to fill the gap, albeit illegally, and began to include marijuana in their inventory of AIDS drugs. By late 1992, cannabis only Buyers' Clubs began to emerge. The movement grew in California, until it again re-emerged in the National spotlight with the passage of Proposition 215, the 1996 ballot initiative that legalized the medical use of marijuana in the state of California.

Compassionate Use Act

Following the passage of California's Prop. 215—
also known as the "Compassionate Use Act"—eight
other states passed medial marijuana laws by citizen's
initiative. As of 2006, there were eleven functional
state medical marijuana programs in the United States,
with support growing for similar programs in states
nationwide.

Common Terms
Defined

Medical marijuana laws are full of legalese—technical jargon used by lawyers to speak to other lawyers and judges. In this chapter, we define the important terms and cover the basic principles and information that medical marijuana patients, caregivers, and physicians should be familiar with.

Knowledge of the following terms is necessary to understand the various state medical marijuana programs, the key players involved in facilitating these programs, and other organizations that provide services to patients.

Patient

A patient is an individual with a qualifying medical condition, whose doctor has written a recommendation or has acknowledged that marijuana may mitigate the symptoms of the patient's medical condition.

Qualifying Condition

Most state programs limit the use of marijuana to patients suffering from certain qualifying medical

conditions. While the qualifying conditions, vary from
state to state, they generally include cancer, glaucoma,
HIV/AIDS, severe pain, multiple sclerosis, and seizure
disorders. In California, any medical condition that
a doctor finds is benefited by marijuana can qualify
a patient, while in other states only two or three
conditions may qualify one to use medical marijuana.
See Chapter 6 for a list of the conditions that can
qualify a patient in each of the different state medical
marijuana programs.

Patient Registry

Some state programs maintain a patient registry
where patients are required to register to become
legally protected to use marijuana. Registry states
usually issue patients registry identification cards,
which serve as proof of a patient's authorization to use
marijuana in that state.

Physician

A patient must be authorized by a physician,
either through a recommendation or through notes in
the patient's medical charts, to use medical marijuana.
A physician may not write a prescription for marijuana,
however, which is explained in Chapter 7. Generally an
authorizing physician generally must be a Doctor of
Medicine (M.D.) or a Doctor of Osteopathic Medicine
(D.O.), and must be licensed to practice in the patient's
state of residence. A physician is not, and may not, act
as a caregiver.

Caregiver

A caregiver is not a medical professional,
but is more like a personal assistant to a patient. This
role may be filled by a friend, relative, or someone else.

Most medical marijuana states recognize the caregiver role and protect it from the state's criminal laws prohibiting possession and cultivation of marijuana.

The caregiver role was created to assist patients with their medical needs, which might include growing, curing, baking, or administering marijuana. Most states require that the caregiver be registered with a designated state agency, which offers protection for the caregiver and allows the state to keep track of who can and who cannot legally possess or grow marijuana.

It is important to note that the role of the caregiver is primarily that of a volunteer. Most states prohibit caregivers from receiving payment for their labors, or for any marijuana they produce. A patient, however, may pay a caregiver for expenses related to growing, such as electricity, soil, fertilizer, and other growing equipment.

Requirements for becoming a caregiver vary from state to state, but most restrictions are based on age and criminal history. See Chapter 10 for requirements and restrictions on caregivers.

Cannabis Clubs

Cannabis clubs—also called cannabis dispensaries—exist almost exclusively in California. The clubs grow or otherwise obtain marijuana and sell it to patients who present proof that they have obtained a doctor's recommendation or approval for medical marijuana use. Some cannabis clubs also hold clinics where potential patients can meet with compassionate doctors for a possible medical marijuana recommendation.

Cannabis clubs are quasi-legal entities allowed to operate in California despite sales of marijuana, which actually violate state law. Cannabis clubs have been subject to federal raids for violation of federal law. There are many cannabis clubs in California, each of which operate uniquely.

Cannabis Cooperatives

Cannabis cooperatives, while similar to the cannabis clubs, are slightly different. The cooperatives are made up of groups of patients who pool resources to grow marijuana, and who split marijuana harvests among members. Members who are physically able generally share in gardening responsibilities.

Cannabis Clinics

Cannabis clinics are non-profit organizations that hold clinics where potential patients can meet with compassionate doctors for a possible medical marijuana recommendation. These clinics assist patients with paperwork, and also provide other support services. Cannabis clinics generally do not sell marijuana.

Legal Basics

W hile a growing number of states have passed medical marijuana laws—also called "statutes", the vast majority of states do not have medical marijuana laws. Even in states without a medical marijuana law, there is some protection, however, by way of what is called "common law." Common law is comprised of the published opinions of various courts; opinions that lawyers can rely upon to defend a client. For example, *Roe v. Wade*, the famous reproductive rights case is common law. It was not passed by legislators, it was decided by judges.

People who do not live in a state with a medical marijuana statute may still be able to find legal protection for medical marijuana use by presenting a common law defense known as the "medical necessity defense." In fact, even in states with medical marijuana laws, it is sometimes still possible to present a medical necessity defense if the statutory protection is not sufficient to meet a patient's medication needs.

Federal Law v. State Law

To understand medical marijuana law, it is necessary to know a little bit about the principle of federalism, and how state and federal laws in the United States work both together and independently.

The federal government and the individual state governments are distinct entities, each responsible for legislating over different realms. The federal government is limited to regulating issues of national import while states are allowed to regulate only within their borders. Occasionally, these realms intersect, creating the potential for a conflict of laws. While a state may pass laws that regulate activities within its borders, if the federal government passes a law regulating the same activity, the federal law supersedes state law. This is a principle of the Supremacy Clause of the United States Constitution.

The Supremacy Clause of the US Constitution holds that Federal law supersedes state law.

Commerce Clause

Determining when state law applies and when federal law applies is an on-going challenge addressed by our judicial system. In the sphere of medical marijuana, this conflict has centered on a clause of the Constitution known as the Commerce Clause. The Commerce Clause, as written in the Constitution, simply states that "the Congress shall have Power...to regulate Commerce with foreign Nations, and among the several States, and with the Indian Tribes." It is a short and simple clause as written, but is one of the more contentious areas of constitutional law.

The federal Controlled Substances Act, which prohibits all uses of marijuana, is premised on the Commerce Clause. Congress claimed the power to regulate the local use and growing of marijuana based on the ground that all marijuana found in interstate commerce was once local. So, in order to control the interstate commerce in marijuana, the federal government must also control local marijuana.

The federal government's claimed power to regulate local marijuana under the Commerce Clause was challenged by two patients in 2002, and was heard by the Supreme Court on November 29, 2004, in a case called *Gonzalez v. Raich* (2005).

Gonzalez v. Raich

On August 12, 2002, agents from the DEA and local sheriff's department raided the home of Diane Monson. Ms. Monson suffers from a painful and degenerative back condition and was growing six plants inside her home as permitted by California's medical marijuana law. As a lawful medical marijuana user under state law, the sheriff's deputies determined that her garden was legal and then left. But, the DEA agents were there to enforce federal law, which recognizes no medical marijuana exceptions. The DEA agents seized Ms. Monson's plants and destroyed them.

Ms. Monson, in partnership with Angel McClary Raich, a medical marijuana user who suffers from several debilitating medical conditions, including an inoperable brain tumor, sued the federal government. In their suit, the two women sought a court order that would bar enforcement of the federal Controlled Substances Act against patients who use marijuana in compliance with state law and without engaging in any interstate activity.

They argued that only state law can regulate "the intrastate, non-commercial cultivation, possession, and use of marijuana for personal medical purposes on the advice of a physician and in accordance with state law." Such use, the women argued, had nothing to do with "commerce" and took place entirely within one state—California. Thus, they argued, the federal government had no power to prohibit such activity under the Commerce Clause.

Gonzales v. Raich was decided in the summer of 2005. The Supreme Court ruled against the women, upholding the constitutionality of federal marijuana prohibition even as applied to medical marijuana patients who grow, possess, or use marijuana entirely within the borders of a medical marijuana state.

Marijuana is like Wheat

The court, in ruling against Raich and Monson, relied primarily on a 1942 Supreme Court case, *Wickard v. Filburn*, which dealt with a federal law regulating the production of wheat. The 1938 law regulated how much wheat a farmer could grow, and instituted penalties against farmers who exceeded this limit. Filburn, a wheat farmer, produced wheat for market within these regulations, but produced wheat in excess of those limits for private use by his family.

In *Wickard*, the court declared that, although the excess wheat was grown intrastate for non-commercial home-consumption, the aggregate impact of this practice had a substantial effect on interstate commerce, thus bringing it within the scope of the federal commerce power. In essence, the court reasoned that the fact that Filburn produced excess wheat for home consumption negatively affected the market price for wheat because Filburn did not have to purchase wheat from the marketplace, and therefore his excess production would undermine the purpose of the federal regulatory law.

Similarly, in *Raich*, the Supreme Court found that the home cultivation and consumption of marijuana, although not introduced into commerce, would affect the illicit trade in marijuana, because patients would not be purchasing marijuana from the black market, or because unscrupulous patients might divert legally produced marijuana into the black market.

Significance of *Raich*

While the *Raich* case was a victory for the federal government and a loss for patients, the actual impact of the case on medical marijuana users is very limited.

State Protection is Not Federal Protection

The decision does not affect the legality of any of the existing state programs or prevent other states from creating their own medical marijuana programs. Rather, the decision simply reasserts the power of the federal government to regulate marijuana, including its medical use, pursuant to the Commerce Clause. This means that the federal government has the power to prosecute patients and caregivers even in states that have passed medical marijuana programs. Although the federal government has this power, as a practical matter the feds usually don't have the time, resources, or incentive to prosecute individual medical marijuana patients.

The threat of individual users being busted is minimal because the federal government is more inclined to target cannabis dispensaries and large grow operations, which are likely to net at least one hundred plants or one hundred kilos of marijuana—the amount necessary to impose a five-year mandatory minimum sentence under federal law. While federal prosecution continues to be a possibility, it is a slim possibility—only about 1% of all marijuana arrests each year are made by federal agents.

Some members of Congress, especially those representing states that have adopted medical marijuana laws, are working to give patients more protection against federal prosecution. In 2005, a bipartisan group of legislators introduced the *Steve*

McWilliams Truth in Trials Act, a bill that would allow
individuals being prosecuted under federal drug laws to
offer evidence that they were in compliance with state
laws allowing the medical use of marijuana. While not
a perfect fix, nor a codification of the medical necessity
defense, such a bill would provide much needed
security for patients who live in medical marijuana
states. Unfortunately, it still leaves patients in non-
medical marijuana states out in the cold.

Raich's Impact on Travel

Although the *Raich* case did not explicitly
address the right to travel, one
implication of the case is that
it is a federal crime to travel
between states in possession of
medical marijuana. Travel *within*
a state is regulated by state law,
whereas travel *between* states is
entirely regulated by federal law.
Because the federal government
does not recognize medical marijuana, it is a federal
crime to possess medical marijuana while traveling
from one state to the next, *even if both states have
medical marijuana laws*. There are some constitutional
problems with this, but they have yet to be decided by
any court.

*Travel within a
state is regulated
by state law,
whereas travel
between states is
entirely regulated
by federal law.*

The Medical Necessity Defense

I f a patient who benefits from marijuana does not qualify under a state program, or lives in a state that doesn't recognize medical marijuana, the patient *might* be able to use a "medical necessity" defense. A medical necessity defense is a common law defense (like self-defense) that can be raised in court in response to criminal charges. The medical necessity defense is derived from the common law doctrine of "necessity." The necessity doctrine allows an accused individual to argue that, due to an imminent danger to himself or a loved one, he had no choice but to commit the crime and that breaking the law was, therefore, justified under the circumstances.

To present a necessity defense, a person caught breaking a criminal law argues that less harm was done by breaking the law than by complying with it. The classic example is breaking the speed limit in order to rush someone to the hospital. One common application of the necessity defense has been in prisoner escape cases, where a prisoner defends against a charge of escape by arguing, for example, that the prison was on fire or that another prisoner was about to kill him, and that his escape was therefore necessary to avoid the greater harm of death inside the prison.

United States v. Randall

The first successful use of the medical necessity defense in a marijuana case—indeed the first successful use of *any* medical necessity defense—was in 1976 when Robert Randall was prosecuted for possession of four marijuana plants.

In the case of *United States v. Randall*, Randall, who was battling a severe case of glaucoma, presented evidence to the court that marijuana reduced his intraocular eye pressure, preventing him from going blind, and that the conventional medical treatments available were ineffective at treating his condition (1976). In support of his medical necessity defense, Randall offered the testimony of two doctors who stated that they would prescribe marijuana to Randall if it were legally available. Randall also offered into evidence tests that had been conducted on his eye pressure showing that marijuana reduced the pressure down to normal ranges. This evidence was sufficient to persuade the court that Randall's choice to break the law, by using marijuana, was the only thing preventing him from going blind.

In the court's ruling, the judge explained that three reasons convinced him to accept Randall's medical necessity defense. These reasons laid the groundwork for future use of the medical necessity defense. The elements the judge identified are as follows:

1. Randall did not intentionally bring about the circumstances (Glaucoma) that precipitated the unlawful act (medical use of marijuana);

2. Randall could not accomplish the same objective (preserving his sight) using accepted medical practices; and

3. The evil sought to be avoided (loss of sight) was more serious and harmful than the unlawful act perpetrated to avoid it (medical use of marijuana).

Elements of a Medical Necessity Defense

The elements identified by the judge in *Randall* remain the basic elements of a medical necessity defense today. There are two additional elements included below (1 and 2), to add clarity for the reader, as they are essential to the larger picture of the medical necessity defense. These are the elements that a patient must establish in order to successfully defend against criminal charges by raising a medical necessity defense:

1. The medical necessity defense has not been precluded by legislative action.

2. The harm caused by the patient's condition is not speculative or debatable.

3. The patient's medical condition was not brought about intentionally.

4. The patient could not alleviate his or her condition by conventional medications.

5. The harm that will occur to the patient without medical marijuana must be greater than the harm caused by allowing the patient to use marijuana.

ELEMENT 1: The medical necessity defense has not been precluded by legislative action

As you might imagine, prosecutors do not like the necessity defense, and view it as an end-run around a criminal law. Consequently when a prosecutor learns that a defendant in a marijuana case is planning on raising a medical necessity defense at trial, the prosecutor will often argue that some piece of legislation bars the defense. Usually, the prosecutor will point to the fact that marijuana has been declared a controlled substance by the legislature—one with no accepted medical use—and argue that this shows that the legislature has precluded a medical necessity defense. Some judges accept this reasoning and prohibit defendants in marijuana cases from introducing *any* evidence of medical necessity; others do not.

For example, a Florida Court of Appeals held that although the legislature had placed marijuana in Schedule I of Florida's Controlled Substance Act, this act did *not* preclude a medical necessity defense. Moreover, the court found that the defendants in that case in which a husband and wife who both suffered from AIDS and who were caught growing two marijuana plants, successfully established the defense (*Jenks v. Florida*, 1991).

The opposite outcome occurred in the case of *Minnesota v. Hanson* (1991). In *Hanson*, the Minnesota Court of Appeals was called upon to decide whether an epileptic who used marijuana to control his seizures could be allowed to present a medical necessity defense, or whether the defense had been precluded by legislative action.

The Minnesota legislature had classified marijuana as a Schedule I drug with "no currently accepted medical use." The state legislature had also created a single exception for supervised use of marijuana by cancer patients undergoing chemotherapy, when it created the THC Therapeutic Research Act (TRA) in 1980. Relying on this legislation, the Minnesota Court of Appeals ruled that the state legislature, by creating a very narrow exception for the medical use of marijuana, had excluded the possibility of using a medical necessity defense for any condition not mentioned in the TRA. Because the defendant did not fit into the exception created by the TRA, the court barred him from raising a medical necessity defense.

Similarly, the Supreme Court of New Jersey held that a defendant cannot raise a medical necessity defense to criminal marijuana charges. That court explained, "the legislature has weighed the competing value of medical use of marijuana against the values served by prohibition of its use or possession, and has set forth the narrow circumstances under which that competing value may be served. Outside those narrow circumstances, the value of medical use of marijuana cannot be deemed to outweigh the values served by its prohibition." (*New Jersey v. Tate*, 1986).

At least one appellate court in California has refused to allow a medical necessity defense to marijuana charges, finding that Proposition 215 (The Compassionate Use Act) is the sole means by which a medical defense can be offered. The court stated:

> *Although Proposition 215 establishes a narrow exception to our drug laws for the medical use of marijuana, it does so only for a patient or a patient's primary caregiver, only for the crimes of possession or cultivation of marijuana, and only upon a physician's recommendation or approval. To grant defendant a broader medical necessity defense would eliminate the voters' decision to limit the immunity to only certain crimes, to only a particular class of persons (patients*

*and their primary caretakers), and to only those
patients who had a physician's approval for personal
medical use* (People v. Galambos, 2002).

Likewise, Washington courts allowed medical marijuana
users to present medical necessity defenses, but a
case in 2005 reversed that trend, holding that passage
of Washington's medical marijuana law signaled the
Legislature's intent to close the door on the common
law medical necessity defense (*Washington v. Butler*,
2005).

Nevertheless, there remain many states where this
defense has not been tested. In fact, over thirty state
legislatures have passed laws authorizing general
necessity defenses. These laws should also apply to
medical necessity defenses because medical necessity
is simply a subtype of the general necessity defense.

One state that deserves special mention with regard
to the medical marijuana necessity defense is Maryland.
Maryland is unique in having recognized by statute an
explicit medical marijuana necessity defense. Under
this law, an individual charged with possession of less
than one ounce of marijuana and who has a doctor's
recommendation for medical use, is permitted to
present a necessity defense to the charges. If the
person proves the elements discussed earlier, the court
is limited to fining the person $100, and no criminal
record results.

The Maryland law is odd. It provides no protection
for growing marijuana, and is strictly limited to less
than one ounce of marijuana. Further, it allows the
court to impose a $100 fine even if the person proves
the necessity defense. This doesn't make much sense,
other than as a political compromise.

ELEMENT 2: The harm caused by the patient's condition is not speculative or debatable

The second element, requiring a specific risk of harm to a patient's health, was a significant factor in *Randall*, although it was not listed by the court as an element of the defense. Randall had been diagnosed with glaucoma in 1972, and his doctors believed that treatment with conventional medications would leave him blind within five years.

If Randall had not been diagnosed with glaucoma, but was simply genetically predisposed to develop it, the harm would have been too speculative for the court to consider a medical necessity defense. To use a medical necessity defense the patient must have a diagnosed medical condition that will lead to a specific harm (blindness within five years in the case of Mr. Randall), if not successfully treated.

ELEMENT 3: The patient's medical condition was not brought about intentionally

This element is mostly a holdover from the traditional "necessity" defense, and is generally not relevant in a medical necessity context.

ELEMENT 4: The patient could not alleviate his condition by conventional medications

Satisfying the fourth element requires presentation of medical evidence demonstrating that marijuana use has a beneficial effect on the patient's medical condition, as well as showing that conventional medications and treatment are ineffective in treating the patient's condition. The most helpful evidence will show a history of medications used by the patient that have been tried and either failed to have an effect, or

caused unbearable side-effects. The medical record
should also track the patient's use of marijuana and
any beneficial outcomes that have been produced by
such use. It is best if the patient's primary physician
testifies, but in the case that he is unwilling, another
physician may be found to testify so long as there
is ample information in the medical record that the
physician may base an opinion upon. In any case,
patients need some sort of expert medical testimony
to support their defense.

In 2003, an Illinois judge rejected a woman's request
to present a medical necessity defense to the jury
because she did not prove that marijuana was the "sole
viable alternative." Despite the fact that the woman
had been through forty glaucoma surgeries in twenty-
two years, the judge denied the defense because the
woman had not tried laser surgery (*Gordon*, 2003).
This court was extreme in requiring that marijuana be
the *only* alternative. Other courts, such as the *Randall*
court, have been more flexible and have considered the
severity and the effectiveness of the accepted medical
treatments when deciding whether or not marijuana
was a necessity.

ELEMENT 5: The harm that will occur to the patient without medical marijuana must be greater than the harm caused by allowing the patient to use marijuana.

This element often turns on political geography
or the political temperament of the judge more than
anything else. There are some judges who believe
that marijuana is extremely dangerous to users and
to society. With this perspective, it can be an uphill
fight to convince the judge that a greater harm will
come from prohibiting the patient from using medical
marijuana. The case of *Commonwealth v. Hutchins*
perfectly illustrates this unfortunate reality (1991).

In *Hutchins*, the Supreme Judicial Court of Massachusetts ruled that Hutchins could not use a medical necessity defense even if the court were to accept the severity of his medical condition as described in affidavits to the court. Hutchins, who suffers from scleroderma, a chronic disease that causes build-up of scar tissue throughout the body, submitted portions of his medical records to the court detailing "episodes of fatigue, hypertension, loss of appetite, weight loss of up to twenty-five pounds, diarrhea, nausea, vomiting ... constriction of the esophagus, extreme difficulty and pain in swallowing, and swollen, painful joints," caused by his medical condition.

Hutchins' condition was so extreme at one point that a doctor recommended surgery to treat his severely constricted esophagus by surgically removing the esophagus and replacing it with a portion of his intestine. The court, although accepting the submitted evidence pertaining to Hutchins' medical condition and the medical efficacy of marijuana in treating his condition, rejected his medical necessity defense. The court stated that it could not "dismiss the reasonably possible negative impact of such a judicial declaration on the enforcement of our drug laws, including but not limited to those dealing with marihuana, nor can we ignore the government's overriding interest in the regulation of such substances."

This element is the least predictable in terms of success, but should not deter patients from asserting a medical necessity defense.

Common Law
"Necessity" Defense

While the medical necessity defense is by no means a magical safety-net, it remains a viable option for patients in many circumstances when no state protection is available for the medical use of marijuana. If the medical necessity defense is unsuccessful, a patient may be able to fallback on the conventional "necessity" defense.

In *Idaho v. Hastings*, an Idaho woman was arrested for growing twelve marijuana plants in her basement (1990). The woman, who suffered from rheumatoid arthritis and used marijuana to control related pain and muscle spasms, requested that the jury be instructed on the medical necessity defense. The trial court refused to allow the medical necessity defense, which had not previously been recognized in Idaho, a decision that was affirmed by the Idaho Supreme Court. However, the Supreme Court allowed the woman to return to trial to argue the common law defense of necessity instead.

The elements of the necessity defense are similar to those of the medical necessity defense and include the following requirements:

1. That there be a specific threat of immediate harm;

2. That the circumstances which require the illegal act were not instigated by the defendant;

3. That the same objective could not have been accomplished by a legal or less offensive alternative available to the defendant;

4. That the harm caused by the illegal act was not worse or disproportionate to the harm avoided.

If your state has previously disallowed, or currently disallows, the medical necessity defense then the common law necessity defense may be a viable alternative, as the *Hastings* case illustrates.

Federal Medical Necessity

Federally, the experience with the medical necessity defense is somewhat different. Since 1980, necessity defenses have been permitted to federal offenses—with the exception of murder. In that year, the United States Supreme Court permitted a necessity defense in a prison escape case where the prisoners argued that escaping was necessary because the guards were dangerous and were engaging in reckless behavior that threatened to burn the prison down. The Supreme Court allowed the prisoners to present evidence of necessity, although in the end the Court upheld the prisoners' convictions for escape after finding that escaping was not their only alternative (*United States v. Bailey*, 1980).

Only two federal cases directly address a medical necessity defense to federal marijuana possession charges, the first of which was *United States v. Burton* (1990). While *United States v. Oakland Cannabis Buyers' Cooperative*, described below, was decided later, *Burton* is the only other federal case that patients and attorneys can look to for any direction on presenting a medical necessity defense. It thus merits brief discussion.

In *Burton*, James Burton was charged with growing marijuana and possession with intent to distribute in violation of federal law. At trial, he was allowed to argue that he used marijuana out of medical necessity to treat his glaucoma. While Burton was able to avoid conviction for growing and possession with intent to distribute, he was convicted of three

counts of possession, a lesser charge. Burton appealed
his conviction to the Sixth Circuit Court of Appeals,
arguing that the jury's verdict was inconsistent with
the evidence.

The Sixth Circuit acknowledged that "medical
necessity" is a viable defense to a federal charge of
marijuana possession, but found that Burton had not
satisfied the elements of the defense. At the time the
case was decided in 1990, the Federal Investigational
New Drug Program was still operating and ostensibly
available as a legal alternative. Because a legal means
of treating his medical condition was available—i.e.,
enrolling in the Investigational New Drug Program—the
Sixth Circuit refused to revisit Burton's conviction on
medical necessity grounds, and let the possession
conviction stand.

The most important federal case concerning
medical necessity, *United States v. Oakland Cannabis
Buyers' Cooperative*, was decided by the United States
Supreme Court in 2001. The case involved the Oakland
Cannabis Buyers' Cooperative (OCBC), a not-for-
profit organization that provided marijuana to eligible
patients under California's Compassionate Use Act.
After the OCBC refused to comply with a court order
prohibiting it from distributing marijuana, the federal
government initiated contempt proceedings against
the organization. Contempt proceedings are generally
used as a method of disciplining parties who defy court
orders. In its defense, the OCBC contended that its
continued distributions of marijuana were "medically
necessary."

The Supreme Court held that the medical necessity
defense did not apply to circumstances concerning a
cooperative's manufacture or *distribution* of marijuana.
The decision was hailed by the federal government
as a definitive case on the medical necessity defense.

However, for all of the government's rhetoric, the impact of the case was actually very limited.

The Court never addressed the question of whether a *patient* may assert a medical necessity defense to federal charges of possession or cultivation of marijuana. As explained by Justice Stevens in his concurring opinion, "whether the defense might be available to a seriously ill patient for whom there is no alternative means of avoiding starvation or extraordinary suffering is a difficult issue that is not presented here."

Although the question of whether an individual can raise a medical necessity defense to federal marijuana charges was not answered by the Supreme Court, some lower federal courts have exploited the OCBC decision by applying it to individual defendants and preventing them from introducing any evidence of medical necessity. Eventually, one of these cases will likely reach the Supreme Court giving the Court an opportunity—for better or worse—to finally decide whether the medical necessity defense can be raised by individual patients facing federal marijuana charges.

States in Which Courts Refused to Recognize a Marijuana Necessity Defense

Alabama	*Kauffman v. Alabama, 1993*
California	*People v. Galambos, 2002*
Georgia	*Spillers v. Georgia, 1978*
Idaho	*Idaho v. Hastings, 1990*
Maine	*Maine v. Christen, 1997*
Massachusetts	*Commonwealth v. Hutchins, 1991*
Minnesota	*Minnesota v. Hanson, 1991*
New Jersey	*New Jersey v. Tate, 1986*
South Dakota	*South Dakota v. Ducheneaux, 2003*
Virginia	*Murphy v. Com., 1999*
Washington	*Washington v. Butler, 2005*

Qualifying Conditions

States with medical marijuana laws usually specify certain medical conditions that a patient must have to qualify for legal protection, and require some sort of acknowledgment or recommendation from a licensed physician. The doctor's statement generally must specify that marijuana alleviates the medical condition or that it is an appropriate treatment. It also helps if the physician can document that the patient has tried various medications, whether over-the-counter or prescription, and that these medications have proven ineffective or had unacceptable side effects.

The table on the next page lists conditions that can qualify patients in the various state's medical marijuana programs. Some medical conditions, such as cancer and multiple sclerosis, are a qualifying condition in every program while other conditions may only be qualified in one or two states. In some states, simply being diagnosed with the condition is not sufficient; the patient must also meet certain other criteria.

AIDS

AIDS *(Acquired Immune Deficiency Syndrome)* is recognized as a qualifying condition in every medical marijuana state except for Washington. An AIDS diagnosis is sufficient to qualify a patient for

Conditions that can qualify patients for medical marijuana use by states

Qualifying Condition	Alaska	California	Colorado	Hawaii	Maine	Montana	Nevada	Oregon	Rhode Island	Vermont	Washington
AIDS	X	X	X	X	X	X	X	X	X	X	
Alzheimer's Agitation								X	X		
Arthritis		X									
Cachexia*	X	X	X	X	X	X	X	X	X		
Cancer	X	X	X	X	X	X	X	X	X	X	X
Crohn's Disease				X		X		X			
Epilepsy	X	X	X	X	X	X	X	X	X		X
Glaucoma	X	X	X	X	X	X	X	X	X		X
Hepatitis C									X		
HIV	X		X	X		X		X	X	X	X
Migraine		X									
Multiple Sclerosis	X	X	X	X	X	X	X	X	X	X	X
Persistent Muscle Spasms*	X	X	X	X	X	X	X	X	X		
Seizures*	X	X	X	X	X	X	X	X	X		X
Severe Nausea*	X	X	X	X		X	X	X	X		
Severe Pain*	X	X	X	X		X	X	X	X		X
Other illnesses for which mj provides relief		X									

*These conditions are qualifying when symptomatic of a chronic and/or debilitating illness or their respective treatments. See section on "Symptoms of Chronic or Debilitating Illnesses.

protection under the states's medical marijuana law, with the exception of Maine and Vermont.

In order to qualify under Maine's law, an AIDS patient must be suffering from persistent nausea, vomiting, wasting syndrome or loss of appetite resulting from AIDS or its treatment. In Vermont, AIDS patients only qualify if they are experiencing severe, persistent, and intractable symptoms as a result of their condition or its treatment, and if "reasonable medical efforts have been made over a reasonable amount of time without success in relieving the symptoms." In addition, AIDS patients in Vermont qualify if they are receiving end of life care.

Thus, in Maine and Vermont, when diagnosing a patient with AIDS it is important for the physician to document the above-noted symptoms.

Alzheimer's Agitation

Oregon and Rhode Island are the only states that allow the use of medical marijuana to treat agitation related to Alzheimer's Disease.

Arthritis

California is the only state that allows medical use of marijuana for treating arthritis.

Cancer

Cancer is one of only two conditions that qualify patients to be treated with marijuana in every medical marijuana program. However, in Maine and Vermont a diagnosis is not sufficient by itself. Maine limits the use of marijuana to treat persistent nausea, vomiting, wasting syndrome or loss of appetite that results from chemotherapy or radiation therapy.

Cancer patients in Vermont are only eligible to medicate with marijuana if they are experiencing severe, persistent and intractable symptoms as a result of their condition or treatment, and if "reasonable medical efforts have been made over a reasonable amount of time without success in relieving symptoms." Cancer patients may also be eligible in Vermont if they are receiving end of life care, or are otherwise in an advanced stage of the illness. So, again, it is important for the patient's doctor when diagnosing cancer to document these additional qualifying symptoms or conditions.

Crohn's Disease

Crohn's Disease is a chronic and painful inflammatory disease of the digestive tract. It is often accompanied by muscle cramps and spasms, loss of appetite, and severe weight loss. Hawaii, Montana and Rhode Island permit the use of marijuana to treat Crohn's Disease when it is accompanied by persistent muscle spasms or cramping.

Patients who suffer from Crohn's Disease should also be aware that while only Hawaii, Montana and Rhode Island expressly list the disease by name, medical protection is likely available in the other medical marijuana states which permit medical marijuana use for persistent muscle spasms resulting from chronic illness and for wasting syndrome.

Epilepsy

Washington permits use of marijuana to treat epilepsy and other spasticity disorders. With the exception of Vermont, the other ten medical marijuana states permit the use of marijuana to treat seizures associated with epilepsy.

Glaucoma

The first successful medical necessity defense in a marijuana case was raised by Robert Randall, who was suffering from severe glaucoma, a disease in which unusually high pressure in the eye damages the optic nerve leading to loss of vision. With the exception of Vermont, glaucoma is considered a qualifying condition that permits the patient to use marijuana in all of the other states with medical marijuana programs.

Washington is also more restrictive than other states, allowing treatment with marijuana only in *acute* or *chronic* cases where increased eye pressure can't be relieved by standard treatments and medications. However, what exactly is meant by "acute" or "chronic" is left undefined by the law. For glaucoma sufferers in Washington seeking to qualify for medical marijuana treatment it is important for the patient's doctor to document the severity of the disease and the age at which it first afflicted the patient.

Hepatitis C

Rhode Island is the only state that permits the use of marijuana in the treatment of Hepatitis C.

HIV

HIV (*Human Immunodeficiency Virus*) is the virus that causes AIDS. HIV attacks the immune system, increasing the person's susceptibility to other infections. Many people who have been infected with HIV suffer only mild to moderate symptoms.

With the exception of Maine and Nevada, all of the medical marijuana states consider HIV a qualifying condition. Vermont, being more restrictive than other states, limits medical marijuana use to HIV patients experiencing severe, persistent and intractable symptoms as a result of their condition or treatment, and to situations where reasonable medical efforts have been made over a reasonable amount of time without success in relieving symptoms. California does not explicitly list HIV as a qualifying condition, but it can still be the basis for qualifying for medical marijuana use because California also protects "any other illness for which marijuana provides relief." Patients suffering from HIV should speak with their doctor about obtaining a recommendation.

Migraine

California is the only state that allows migraines to be treated with marijuana.

Multiple Sclerosis

All medical marijuana states permit the use of marijuana to treat persistent muscle spasms associated with multiple sclerosis. Being more restrictive, Vermont limits medical marijuana use to MS patients experiencing severe, persistent and intractable symptoms as a result of their condition or treatment, and only if symptoms have been unrelieved by more traditional medical methods.

Symptoms of Chronic or Debilitating Illnesses

Certain conditions are treatable under the specified state programs when they occur as symptoms of chronic or debilitating illnesses, such as cachexia associated with HIV/AIDS, or seizures associated with epilepsy. California's more liberal law is the only one that recognizes these conditions and does not require that they be symptomatic of a specified serious illness.

Cachexia

Cachexia, known as "wasting syndrome," is an unfortunate symptom of a wide range of chronic and debilitating illnesses, and can be a side effect of some prescription medications. All the state medical marijuana laws treat wasting syndrome as a qualifying medical condition, with the exception of the more restrictive states of Washington and Vermont.

Because wasting syndrome can occur as a result of many serious illnesses, inclusion of it as a qualifying condition opens the doors to many people who might not have any of the more specific disease diagnoses. This creates a kind of loophole for patients suffering from a chronic or debilitating illness, or taking prescription medications to treat such a condition, which leaves them with a reduced appetite or which otherwise causes a significant loss of weight. Such people, with *careful* documentation, can be an exception, which would likely qualify under the state's medical marijuana law.

In Maine, which is also on the more restrictive end of the continuum, wasting syndrome may only be treated with marijuana if it results from chemotherapy or radiation therapy in the treatment of cancer, or from AIDS or its treatment.

Persistent Muscle Spasms

Individuals who experience persistent muscle spasms as a symptom of a chronic or debilitating illness—or as a result of the treatment of such a condition—may use marijuana as a medical treatment in all medical marijuana states except Vermont and Washington. As with cachexia or wasting syndrome, persistent muscle spasms are not unique to any one disease or illness. Thus, outside of Vermont and Washington, a person suffering from muscle spasms and cramps may qualify for other state programs despite not having any of the specific medical disease diagnoses listed in the state's medical marijuana law.

Seizures

With the sole exception of Vermont, individuals who experience seizures as a symptom of a chronic or debilitating illness (or as a result of the treatment of such a condition) may use marijuana as a medical treatment in their medical marijuana programs. While seizures are commonly equated with epilepsy, they can occur due to other causes. As long as a patient's doctor has documented that the patient has a history of seizures, whether diagnosed as epilepsy or not, that patient has a qualifying condition that can be treated with medical marijuana.

Severe Nausea

A wide range of illnesses and prescription medications can leave a person with severe nausea. With the exception of Maine, Vermont, and Washington, people who experience severe nausea as a symptom of a chronic or debilitating illness (or as a result of the treatment of such a condition) may use marijuana as a medical treatment in the remaining medical marijuana programs.

Severe Pain

Excepting in Maine and Vermont, individuals who suffer severe pain as a symptom of a chronic or debilitating illness (or as a result of the treatment of such a condition) may use marijuana as a medical treatment in most medical marijuana programs. The state of Washington limits the use of marijuana to treat what it terms "intractable pain," which is pain that is unrelieved by standard treatments and medications.

Other Illness

California's medical marijuana law is unique because in addition to protecting a list of medical conditions it also includes a catchall provision. Under this special provision, patients can qualify if they suffer from "any other illness for which marijuana provides relief." This compassionate clause has allowed many Californians to use marijuana to treat such things as back pain, Crohn's Disease, menstrual cramps, stress, and depression, none of which were explicitly listed as qualifying conditions.

California's Compassionate Use Act was clarified in 2003 with the passage of passage of California Senate Bill 420, known as the Medical Marijuana Program Act. The new Act suggests that physicians limit their medical marijuana recommendations to patients who suffer from chronic or persistent medical conditions that either (1) substantially limit the ability of the patient to conduct one or more major life activities (as defined in the Americans with Disabilities Act of 1990) *or* (2) if left unalleviated, may cause serious harm to the patient's safety or physical or mental health.

The reference to the Americans with Disabilities Act of 1990 is tautological. That Act, does not list specific "disabilities." Rather the Act broadly defines a disability as "a physical or mental impairment that substantially limits a major life activity." These are determined on a case-by-case basis.

Finding a Doctor

F inding a doctor who will support a patient's use of medical marijuana is the first step to becoming a legal medical marijuana patient. Many doctors remain skeptical of marijuana's medical value, some are against it for political reasons, and others are afraid of potential legal repercussions. Many patients may be uncomfortable discussing marijuana use with a family doctor, who may view marijuana use as criminal, despite the medical context.

A qualified patient can waste a lot of time and money trying to find a doctor who is sympathetic and willing to help patients qualify for their state program. Non-profit cannabis clinics have popped up in several states, including Oregon, Washington and Hawaii, which provide patients with an opportunity to meet with an open-minded physician. These clinics generally require patients to submit medical records that evidence their qualifying condition.

When a patient is determined to be eligible for the state program they are given an appointment with one of the clinic's doctors. Generally, the doctor will meet with the patient, review his or her medical records, and note that the patient has a qualifying medical condition that may be mitigated by use of marijuana.

What I Need From My Doctor

Patients generally need medical records from their physicians that include a diagnosis of a qualifying medical condition, and/or a note from the physician to the effect that marijuana may mitigate the symptoms of the qualified medical condition. Patients in states with patient registry programs will likely need to submit copies of these documents to a designated state agency to register with the state, and thus become a legal patient. Patients in non-registry states should generally have these documents on hand as proof of their legal use of medical marijuana.

What doctors need to provide varies depending on the state. In some states this will be a recommendation from your doctor or an acknowledgement by your doctor that marijuana may be an effective treatment. In other states you might merely need a diagnosis of a qualifying condition.

Don't Request a "Prescription"

There is a common misconception that a doctor can write a patient a "prescription" for marijuana. This, however, is not the case. Doctors must have a license from the federal government to be able to write a patient any prescription. With this license comes certain rules, one being that a doctor cannot prescribe Schedule I drugs. Marijuana is a Schedule I drug. Were a doctor to write a prescription for marijuana, the doctor's license to prescribe would be revoked.

This is the precise problem that has been encountered in Arizona, after the state passed a well-intentioned but poorly worded medical marijuana initiative in 1996 allowing doctors to "prescribe" any Schedule I controlled substance. So while the voters of

Arizona have approved the medical use of marijuana, no one in the state can actually qualify as a patient because of federal restrictions on doctors' prescription powers.

The states with functional marijuana programs have worked around this legal issue by allowing doctors to qualify patients by giving a patient a "recommendation" or "approval" for medical marijuana use, or by simply noting in the patient's medical record that marijuana mitigates the symptoms of the patient's condition.

States Requiring Physician's Recommendation or Approval

Under California's Compassionate Use Act, a patient needs a written or oral recommendation or approval of a physician. The physician must determine that the person's health would benefit from the use of marijuana in the treatment of the patient's medical condition. The physician does not need to be the patient's primary care physician. While it's best to get your doctor's approval or recommendation in writing, it is not necessary in California. An oral recommendation is sufficient so long as the doctor has made notes in the patient's medical files documenting his or her approval of marijuana as a treatment for the patient's condition. Having a written recommendation or approval is handy, however, because it gives you something to show a police officer should you ever be stopped for a marijuana offense.

By allowing doctors to merely "approve" of a patient's medical marijuana use, California's law takes pressure off physicians because rather than having to formally "recommend" that a patient use marijuana, the doctor can merely approve of such use by a patient.

States Requiring a Signed Physician's Statement

In Alaska, patients must obtain a *signed written document* from their physicians saying that the patient was examined as part of an ongoing doctor-patient relationship, that the patient has been diagnosed with one of the medical conditions covered by Alaska's medical marijuana law, and that the doctor has "considered" other approved medications for treatment of the patient's condition.

In Colorado, Maine, Montana, Nevada, Oregon, and Washington, patients must obtain a *signed written document* from their physicians or *copies of medical records* that support a patient's use of medical marijuana. Each state requires that the statement or medical records contain particular information in order for the patient to receive protection under state law for the medical use of marijuana.

In Colorado, the physician must make notes in his statement, or in the patient's medical records, to the effect that "the patient might benefit from the medical use of Marijuana." Colorado requires that the patient and physician retain an on-going relationship. Patients who change physicians are required to notify the state.

In Maine, the medical records or physician's statement must demonstrate that the physician discussed the possible health risks and benefits of using marijuana with the patient and that the physician provided the patient with a professional opinion concerning the balance of risks and benefits of using marijuana medically. The medical record or statement must also demonstrate that the patient may benefit from the medical use of marijuana, and that the patient will continue to receive care from the same physician. Copies of medical records must be authenticated if used to support a patient's medical use.

In Montana, physicians must note in their statement, or in the patient's medical records, that the "potential benefits of the medical use of marijuana would likely outweigh the health risks" for the patient. Montana requires that this statement be made in the course of a bona-fide physician-patient relationship after a full assessment of the patient's medical history has been completed.

In Nevada, physicians must note in their statement, or in the medical records, that "the medical use of marijuana may mitigate the symptoms or effects of (the patient's) condition," and that the "physician has explained the possible risks and benefits of the medical use of marijuana."

Under the Oregon law, a patient must obtain medical records or a signed written statement from the person's attending physician stating that the patient has been diagnosed with one of the medical conditions covered by Oregon's medical marijuana law, and that the patient's use of medical marijuana may mitigate the symptoms or effects of the patient's medical condition.

Under Washington law, the medical records or physician's statement must evidence that the patient was advised by his physician about the risks and benefits of the medical use of marijuana, as well as having been advised by his physician that he may benefit from the medical use of marijuana. In addition, the medical records or statements must demonstrate the physician's professional opinion that the patient may benefit from the medical use of marijuana.

States Requiring Both Medical Records and a Signed Physician's Statement

Only Rhode Island requires that patients obtain both of these documents from their physician. Rhode Island requires physicians to declare in their statement that "in the practitioner's professional opinion the potential benefits of the medical use of marijuana would likely outweigh the health risks for the qualifying patient." Like Montana, Rhode Island also requires that this statement be made in the course of a bona-fide physician-patient relationship after a full assessment of the patient's medical history has been completed.

States Requiring Physician Certification

Hawaii requires physicians to certify "in writing that, in the physician's professional opinion, the potential benefits of the medical use of marijuana would likely outweigh the health risks for the particular qualifying patient." The physician must then submit the certification and register the patient with the state.

States Requiring a Diagnosis Only

Vermont is the only state where a diagnosis of a qualifying condition is sufficient. The patient does not need a recommendation from his doctor to register with the state, however, the state will contact the patient's physician for verification of the patient's diagnosis. Vermont requires that the physician-patient relationship spans at least six months, and also includes a complete assessment of the patient's medical history and a personal physical exam.

Patient Registry

Medical marijuana programs can be divided into two categories, those with patient registries and those without. The majority of the eleven states—Alaska, Colorado, Hawaii, Montana, Nevada, Oregon, Rhode Island, and Vermont—have some sort of patient registry, requiring a prospective patient to submit paperwork to the state to become legal to use, possess, or grow marijuana for medicinal purposes. Usually this includes documentation obtained from the patient's physician in the form of a physician's statement or medical records.

In addition to submitting a physician's statement and/or medical records, the application process in registry states usually requires submission of personal information, including contact information for the attending physician and personal information for any individual acting as a caregiver for the patient. Each registry state has its own forms that need to be filled out, which are available through the relevant government agency, typically the Department of Health Services.

Once the relevant governmental department has determined that an applicant qualifies for participation in the program, the state will issue the patient a unique registry identification card. This card acts as evidence of the patient's legal right to use marijuana, and allows law enforcement to verify the patient's legal status.

Registry programs also have a system for police officers to verify a patient's status. A well-trained officer should do this before responding to a tip on a marijuana growing operation to insure they are not busting a patient who is legally permitted to grow medical marijuana. Usually this system is composed of a registry database that law enforcement may access for the limited purpose of verifying that a patient is lawfully in possession of marijuana. Law enforcement is not allowed, and generally is unable, to peruse these databases for profiling purposes or for insuring that patients are in compliance with state law. In fact, unauthorized disclosure of patient information by state officials is considered a crime in the states of Montana and Rhode Island. Patients in other states should pressure their legislators to provide the same criminal penalty for unauthorized disclosure.

Non-registry states, which include Maine and Washington, do not require that a patient file any personal information with the state. As a result, patients in these states never receive an official stamp of approval—e.g., a registry identification card—that lets law enforcement know that a patient is in legal possession of marijuana. Patients in these states should carry written paperwork or medical records, from their doctors with them that they can provide to police officers as proof of legitimate medical use.

California does not require registration, but it offers a registration program for patients who would prefer to have some sort of official document indicating that they are qualified medical marijuana users. California likewise has a system for law enforcement to verify the status of registered caregivers.

The various registry programs allow patients to participate in the program for a year at a time, requiring patients to submit updated medical records each year to renew their legal status. While non-registry states don't require renewals, patients in these states should keep records less than a year old on hand as evidence of their medical condition and continued need for medical marijuana.

Patients who recover from an illness, or who no longer qualify under state criteria permitting the medical use of marijuana, are required by registry states to return their registry identification cards and dispose of any leftover marijuana. Patients in non-registry states are also expected to cease growing marijuana and dispose of all marijuana.

Fraud

While a larger debate on the legalization of marijuana in the United States is long overdue, the medical marijuana programs are strictly for qualified medical patients and are not intended to provide legal protection for "recreational" users. The government likes to argue that medical marijuana is simply a front for legalization—a contention that has made it more difficult for legitimate patients to obtain medical marijuana and has subjected many patients to public scorn for their medical choices.

In order to limit the protections of the medical marijuana programs to people who really do have medical problems, several states—California, Colorado, Hawaii, Montana, Rhode Island and Washington—have enacted specific fraud offenses related to medical marijuana. These fraud offenses are in addition to whatever marijuana offense was committed. For example, if a person in any of these states is growing marijuana with a fraudulent medical approval, the person is subject to prosecution for both fraud *and* illegal cultivation.

There are two types of fraud addressed: (1) fraudulently obtaining a medical marijuana registry identification card, and (2) fraudulently representing oneself to a police officer as a valid medical marijuana patient.

In California and Colorado it is a punishable offense to use fraudulent means to obtain a registry identification card from the state, or to fraudulently represent oneself to a police officer as a valid medical marijuana patient. In California, offenders may be jailed for up to six months and fined $1000. A second such offense boosts jail time to one year. In addition, the court can prohibit the person from re-registering for up to six months.

In Hawaii, Montana, Rhode Island and Washington it is a punishable offense to fraudulently represent oneself to a police officer as a valid medical marijuana patient. Actions that will generally be considered fraudulent include stealing or fraudulently using the identification card of another, counterfeiting an identification card, tampering with an identification card or other pertinent record for the purpose of having it accepted as valid documentation permitting the medical use of marijuana, knowingly or purposely fabricating or misrepresenting a registry identification card to a law enforcement officer, and fraudulently representing circumstances relating to the medical use of marijuana to avoid arrest or prosecution.

In Washington, such fraud is classified as a felony. In Hawaii, it is considered a misdemeanor and is subject to a fine of $500. In Montana, any person convicted of fraudulent representation of medical use of marijuana can be fined up to $1,000 and placed in jail for up to six months. In Rhode Island, fraudulent representation to a law enforcement official is punishable by a fine of five hundred dollars.

Caregivers

The role of caregiver is essential to medical marijuana programs. Without legal protection for caregivers medical marijuana patients would be forced to buy marijuana on the street or forced to grow and prepare medicine themselves. Both tasks can be difficult for patients who are disabled or seriously ill.

By recognizing caregivers, medical marijuana programs permit patients to choose an individual whom they trust, and whom the state will then recognize and legally protect, to assist in the production and preparation of medical marijuana. Depending on the state, this role is labeled as 'primary caregiver' or 'designated primary caregiver,' but we simply refer to the role as "caregiver," for clarity sake.

Finding a Caregiver

Finding a caregiver can be a difficult task, compounded by prohibitions on payment to caregivers and by unscrupulous individuals who seek a "caregiver" label for legal protection to grow marijuana for their own use or financial gain. There are few benefits in serving as a caregiver, other then knowing that one is conferring a tremendous benefit on someone who is ill. Thus, it is probably best for patients to start their search within their circle of family and friends.

While all patients want to have a successful crop and an adequate supply of medicine, seeking out a caregiver who is a stranger should be done with caution. It is a relationship that should never be rushed into. While family members or close friends may not be expert cultivators, they can learn how through classes and reading, and will generally always be the safest bet for caregivers.

Only if a patient is unable to cultivate for him or herself, and no family member or friend is willing, capable, or trustworthy enough to be a caregiver, should a patient seek the help of an unknown party. The best place for a patient to start is to meet with other patients who have successful relationships with their caregivers, and to inquire if that person's caregiver would be willing to take on another patient. Depending on the state, however, caregivers may be restricted as to the number of patients they may provide for. A personal referral of this sort is probably the safest bet for using an unknown individual as a caregiver. Of course, a patient will want to establish a personal level of trust before making any final decisions, this may include spending time with the other individual, or taking them out to lunch from time to time. Patients should remember that they confer a major legal right when they designate a caregiver, and that such a designation should not be taken lightly.

Caregiver Qualifications

While almost anyone can be a caregiver, there are three general restrictions on caregivers that are imposed by the different medical marijuana programs. These include: (1) restrictions on age; (2) restrictions on criminal history; and (3) requirements that the caregiver provide patients with a designated minimum standard of care.

Age and Criminal Conviction Limits

Under every of the state program, a caregiver must be at least 18 years old, but in a handful of states the caregiver must be older. In Alaska, Rhode Island and Vermont, caregivers must be at least 21 years old.

Alaska, Montana, Nevada, and Rhode Island, also prohibit individuals with felony drug convictions from serving as caregivers. In Vermont, this restriction applies to anyone with a "drug related conviction," regardless of whether the conviction was for a misdemeanor or felony offense. Alaska also prohibits individuals currently on parole or probation from serving as a caregiver.

Standard of Care Requirements

Six of the medical marijuana states require that caregivers provide a minimum level of care for their patients. The level of care, however, is often poorly defined and thus open to interpretation. For example, in Colorado, Nevada, and Oregon, a caregiver must have "significant responsibility for managing the well-being" of a registered patient. While in California, Maine, and Washington, a caregiver must be someone who "has consistently assumed responsibility for the housing, health, or safety" of the patient. In Maine there is an exception to these responsibilities if the caregiver resides in the same household as the patient.

Growers v. Caregivers

In most of the states, caregivers are permitted to grow medical marijuana for their patient. But, Oregon takes a different approach creating a special role of "grower." The advantage of the Oregon approach is that it permits specialization. Caregivers can concentrate on providing medical care to their patients without having to worry about perfecting their cultivation skills and an expert grower can focus completely on growing the best plants possible.

The downside of Oregon's approach is that a caregiver, who will be growing plants is not protected unless the patient designates the caregiver *both* as caregiver *and* grower. If the roles will be split between two people, then the patient must designate one person as caregiver and the other person as the grower.

Under the Oregon law, the patient must provide the Oregon Department of Human Services with the grower's information, after which the grower is issued a special registration card which must be posted at the grow site. A designated grower may grow marijuana for up to four registered patients at a time, and must post a grow site registration card for *each* patient for whom they grow. A grower who ceases to produce marijuana for a patient, or who has been requested by the patient to return the grow site registration card, must promptly return the registration card and provide all remaining marijuana to the patient at that time.

Becoming a Caregiver

Steps to become a caregiver depend on the state program. Generally, registry states require patients to name an individual as caregiver in their application to the state's medical marijuana program, or in some kind of written notification. This allows the state to run a background check, if required by law, and allows the state to verify a caregiver as a legitimate grower in response to law enforcement inquiries.

Caregivers in Registry States

Some states require patients to register. In these registry states, patients are usually given the option of designating a caregiver on their registration application. If they do so, their caregiver receives a registry identification card similar to the one issued to patients, identifying them as a lawful caregiver. By this method a caregiver who has been designated by a registered patient has some security against future arrest. In the event the caregiver has a run-in with police, they can show their identification card as evidence of their caregiver status.

In Colorado and Hawaii, the state keeps information on registered caregivers in their registry database, which is accessible by law enforcement for verification purposes, but does not issue identification cards to caregivers. This means that should a caregiver in either state be stopped or investigated by law enforcement they will not have the benefit of a card to identify them, but will ultimately be vindicated when their status is verified with the state.

While some states allow patients to designate just about anyone they choose as their caregiver, several of the registry states are more rigorous in their requirements. In Nevada, a caregiver must be approved by the patient's attending physician. Once approval has been obtained it must be submitted to the state in writing before a caregiver may be issued an identification card and begin legally caring for a patient. In Vermont, a potential caregiver must apply to the state for the position, have a criminal background check, and must register with the state as a caregiver. Hawaii also requires caregivers to register.

Caregivers in Non-Registry States

The non-registry programs, of which there are two, each have unique approaches to qualifying a caregiver for legal protection. In Maine, a patient must designate the caregiver, by name, in a written individual instruction or power of attorney for health care.

In Washington, caregivers must be designated in writing as caregiver by the patient and must have a copy of the patient's consent form, signed by the doctor. The written designation must occur before the caregiver assumes responsibility for the patient. A caregiver who is arrested without the above documents in possession is legally barred from raising caregiver status as a defense.

Caregivers in Quasi-Registry States

In California, a registry optional state, caregivers of registered patients are not issued identification cards. Instead, they are identified on the patient's own card, and may be verified by law enforcement through the state registry.

Caregivers of non-registered patients are not as easily verified and thus should carry copies of the patient's relevant medical records as well as a written designation as the patient's caregiver, with them to show to law enforcement officers if the need arises. In fact, even a caregiver of a registered patient, would be wise to maintain such independent evidence of caregiver status. During an encounter with police, the more evidence a caregiver can immediately muster of their protected caregiver status the better. This can prevent the unnecessary seizure of plants and equipment, as well as a trip to the police station, while things are sorted out.

Limitations on Caregivers

Many states limit the number of patients a caregiver can have and, conversely, how many caretakers a patient can have. In Hawaii and Vermont, a patient is limited to one caregiver and a caregiver is limited to one patient. In Montana and Nevada, a patient is limited to having one caregiver. The states of Alaska, California, and Washington limit caregivers to serving one patient, with some exceptions.

In Alaska, a caregiver may care for two or more patients if they "are related to the caregiver by at least the fourth degree of kinship by blood or marriage." Additionally, Alaska allows a patient to designate a primary caregiver and an alternate caregiver. Essentially, the alternate caregiver serves as a backup, in case the primary caregiver is unable to serve the patient for some reason. A patient may name only one of each. The designated primary caregiver is issued a caregiver registry card, which must be physically possessed whenever the person is serving as a caregiver. The alternate caregiver may serve as the primary caregiver, in the primary caregiver's absence, so long as the alternate is in physical possession of the primary caregiver's registry card.

In California, a caregiver may care for multiple patients, but only if each patient resides in the same city or county as the caregiver. In Rhode Island, a caregiver may care for up to five qualifying patients at any given time, and each patient may have up to two caregivers. While no other state explicitly provides for this type of patient caregiver/ratio, several states, including Colorado, Maine and Oregon, have not explicitly quantified the numbers of caregivers per patient or patients per caregiver that are permissible.

Caregiver Compensation

Compensating caregivers is a tricky issue. The basic rule in all states is that a caregiver cannot grow or otherwise provide marijuana to a patient for a profit. Doing so—or even appearing to do so—can subject the caregiver to criminal prosecution.

Most of the medical marijuana programs have not addressed what compensation can or cannot be provided to caregivers. The implication is that the caregiver is to serve as a compassionate volunteer.

Indeed, this is a relatively safe model for thinking about the basic do's and don'ts of compensating a caregiver.

Volunteers are expected to donate their time and skills, but aren't expected to pay money out of their own pockets. In other words, it's reasonable to assume that patients are permitted to pay the expenses of the caregiver. California, Oregon, and Rhode Island make this explicit in their laws.

Payment of expenses can include: paying for necessary growing equipment, such as lights, fertilizer, and hydroponics equipment, along with books, cultivation classes, water, and the utilities necessary for the caregiver to serve the patient's needs. It should also include paying the rent on that portion of a property that the caregiver has devoted to use for the patient.

Growing equipment that is purchased with a patient's money is considered the property of the patient. If the caregiver purchases equipment without compensation from the patient, the equipment remains the property of the caregiver in the event that the patient-caregiver relationship ends.

In most cases, it is best for the patient to directly pay these expenses rather than to reimburse the caregiver. In some cases, however, reimbursing the caregiver is the only practical way. When reimbursing a caregiver for expenses, both the patient and the caregiver should keep detailed receipts and accountings, so that it will later be possible to prove that any exchange of money was purely for expenses and that all the expenses were incurred in order to serve the patient's medical needs.

The medical marijuana laws in California and Montana go a step further. Both states explicitly permit patients to compensate caregivers for their

services. In other words, in these states, a caregiver
need not serve as a volunteer, but instead may receive
"reasonable" compensation for the time and effort put
into serving the patient's needs. What's "reasonable"
is not well defined. At the very least, however, it must
mean that the total amount received by the caregiver
amounts to less than the patient would have paid for
the marijuana if purchased on the street. It is well
known that one effect of marijuana prohibition has been
to drive prices of marijuana artificially high.

Perhaps the best plan for reasonably compensating
the time and effort of a caregiver is for the patient and
caregiver to agree on a set hourly compensation rate,
and for the caregiver to document the hours spent
and provide a compensation statement to the patient
every month or quarter. This makes it clear that the
caregiver is truly being compensated for the time
put into care giving and not being paid for the sale of
marijuana, which is prohibited.

California's Cooperatives and Collectives

The medical marijuana program in California
contains a unique provision that allows an owner
or operator of certain organizations to be named a
caregiver for a patient, as a representative of his or her
organization. The owner, in his place, may designate
up to three employees who will share the role of
caregiver for the patient. The types of organizations
that may step into this role include: clinics, health
care facilities, residential care facilities for the elderly
or for individuals with chronic life-threatening illness,
hospices and home health agencies. Some Cannabis
Clubs in California have set themselves up as caregivers
under this provision, which likely increases their legal
protection so long as they can qualify as one of the
eligible organizations.

California's medical marijuana laws also permit
patients and caregivers to join together with other
patients and caregivers in cooperatives to grow
medical marijuana. Unfortunately, California's law
fails to spell out exactly what can or can't be done
by these collectives. To make matters worse, the
federal government has made it very clear that it
does not recognize the state medical marijuana laws,
and considers medical marijuana collectives to be
tantamount to illegal drug conspiracies in violation of
federal law.

Even within the California courts, the law related to
medical marijuana collectives is actively being hashed
out, largely by brave activists who willingly place
themselves in harms way in order to provide patients
the medicine they need and to help evolve the law.
Anyone who is considering forming a cooperative or
collective in California is encouraged to network with
experienced groups like Americans for Safe Access and
to seek specialized legal advice.

Forms of
Medical Marijuana

Many patients have difficulty growing their own marijuana, or finding a trustworthy caregiver to grow marijuana for them. Relying on the black market for medicine—the traditional source—may not be an option for these patients. Other patients may benefit from marijuana but do not live in a state that recognizes medical marijuana. Many patients are opposed to smoking or cannot smoke for health reasons. Fortunately, there are several alternatives to meet the needs of such patients.

Marinol®, which contains synthetic THC, is available nationwide by prescription. Sativex®, another marijuana based medicine, is in the approval process and may soon become available for prescription. These are both potential alternatives available to patients in states who do not currently have a medical marijuana program, who are unable to obtain marijuana, or who are unable to smoke for health reasons. Additional alternatives to smoking marijuana include oral consumption and vaporization of leaf marijuana.

Marinol®

A doctor can write a prescription for Marinol®, a product manufactured by Unimed Pharmaceutical Company and marketed by Roxane Laboratories, which received FDA approval on December 23, 1992. It contains dronabinol, a synthetic version of D-9-(trans)-tetrahydrocannabinol (THC), the primary active principle of marijuana. Dronabinol received FDA approval in 1985.

The FDA's approval of Marinol® was seen as a concession by the federal government, which was faced with mounting evidence of marijuana's medical value but did not want to make marijuana itself available. Unlike marijuana, which can be grown just about anywhere, Marinol® can be controlled and regulated. By touting Marinol® as the "Pot Pill," the government was able to create the perception that they were legalizing a safe form of medical marijuana, and at the same time quell the growing calls to reschedule marijuana for medicinal purposes.

The Pros

Unlike marijuana, the potency of which can vary based on a myriad of factors, Marinol® is available in standardized doses of 2.5 mg, 5 mg, and 10 mg. Marinol® also has the benefit of being orally ingested, avoiding the need to inhale burning organic matter. Some physicians prefer Marinol® to smoked marijuana because they feel that it is inappropriate for medicine to be administered by smoking—since smoking itself carries adverse health consequences.

Marinol® also has the legal benefit of being an FDA approved drug, so a patient who has a valid prescription for Marinol® need not fear the visits of law enforcement agents. Further, while medical marijuana is only legal in a handful of states—and even in those states it is still illegal under Federal law—Marinol® is fully legal nationwide. Thus a user of Marinol® can travel without risk of being arrested, whereas a medical marijuana user is under a threat of arrest in any state that has not expressly approved medical marijuana.

The Cons

Marinol® is an effective medicine for some, but it is hardly the pharmaceutical equivalent of marijuana. Marijuana is a complex plant with over four hundred chemical constituents, at least sixty of which are considered cannabinoids, not found anywhere else in nature. There are at least three other components of marijuana that have medical properties, each of which appear in marijuana in varying quantities, often depending on the strain and growing conditions of the plant. In addition to THC, these compounds include Cannabidiol (CBD), Cannabinol (CBN), and Δ-8 THC. CBD has properties that include: anti-convulsive, anti-anxiety, anti-psychotic, anti-emetic, anti-inflammatory, anti-oxidant and sedative properties. Perhaps more importantly, CBD helps to regulate and curb the often intense intoxicating effect of THC.

A major problem with Marinol® is the absence of CBD content, a factor that has caused many patients to have intense and unpleasant psychoactive reactions, which CBD helps to minimize in users of the natural plant. As for the other compounds, CBN acts as a potent sedative and Δ-8 THC has similar properties to THC.

Another drawback of Marinol® is the hefty price of between $4.00 and $10.00 per pill. This is a price many patients cannot afford, especially when the same amount of medical marijuana would cost much less. On the other hand, the cost of Marinol® is covered by medical insurance unlike the costs of growing and obtaining marijuana, which are not covered .

Besides being expensive, Marinol® has other downsides. Unlike smoking, which allows patients to adjust their does, a patient taking Marinol® must wait an hour or more for the drug to take effect. As a result it is difficult for patients to adjust their doses to a comfortable level and easy for them to ingest too much without realizing it—which rarely happens with smoked marijuana.

Robert Randall voiced another problem with Marinol® when he asked, "Who, but a bureaucrat, would be dumb enough to give a vomiting patient a pill?" (*Randall & O'Leary*, 1998, p. 262). Marijuana is an effective anti-emetic, but if ingested orally like Marinol®, will generally be thrown up before taking effect. In contrast, smoked marijuana takes effect immediately and cannot be rejected by the body during the digestive process, as Marinol® of is. There is a significant difference in the medical effects of THC taken orally in the form of a pill as compared to THC absorbed through smoking marijuana. Marijuana preparations, like Marinol®, which are orally ingested, produce significantly stronger and longer lasting effects than when marijuana is smoked. Many patients report that the psychoactive effects of Marinol®, or other orally ingested marijuana preparations, are too intense to offer them comfort or relief from their symptoms, which is another reason for Marinol®s limited popularity among doctors.

While Marinol® is a legal prescription medicine in all fifty states and medically effective under some circumstances, patients should not be fooled into thinking that Marinol® is the medical equivalent of marijuana. This is not to say that Marinol® is not an option, or that it won't work for a particular patient, but only that its effect is significantly different from that produced by inhaled marijuana.

Sativex®

Whereas Marinol® is a synthetic THC—and *only* THC, another product named Sativex® is a marijuana-based mouth-spray extracted from cannabis plants grown for a high CBD content, which retains much of the chemical complexity of marijuana. The result is an inhaled spray-form of marijuana that is said to produce little intoxicating effect. The product is produced by GW Pharmaceuticals, a British pharmaceutical firm, and has been approved in Canada for treatment of Multiple Sclerosis patients. While GW Pharmaceuticals is still waiting for approval of Sativex® in Britain, British doctors can apply for a special license to prescribe Sativex® imported from Canada. Sativex® is also being investigated as a treatment for multiple sclerosis and cancer in Catalonia, Spain.

Although Sativex® is not yet available in the U.S., GW Pharmaceuticals received FDA permission on January 4, 2006, to conduct "Phase III" clinical trials into the effectiveness of Sativex® in treating severe pain in cancer patients. The clinical trial, which will involve some 250 patients, is expected to be completed in two or three years. After the completion of the clinical trial, GW Pharmaceuticals will have to apply for FDA approval, a process that could begin as early as 2008. The fact that Sativex® is a plant-based extract may present a roadblock towards FDA approval. On the other hand, Sativex® might be embraced by the federal government in the hopes that it will, much like Marinol®, defuse the growing public support for medical marijuana.

Alternatives to Smoking

An ongoing argument against the medical use of marijuana is that smoked medicine is not good medicine because of inhaled toxins. This position has

been seriously deflated by a 2006 study funded by the
National Institute on Drug Abuse, which found no link
between marijuana smoking and cancers of the lungs,
head or neck. However, it is likely that other dangers
associated with smoking remain, such as emphysema.
Fortunately, there are alternatives to smoking
marijuana that are just as effective.

Oral Consumption

Oral ingestion of marijuana offers patients a
healthy alternative to smoking. Eating marijuana in
cookies and other foods has the benefit of providing
relief for a longer period of time, which may be useful
in circumstances where patients are not able to smoke
for an extended period of time, such as when a patient
is traveling, running errands, or involved in activities
away from home. Many patients prefer "edibles," as
they are called, to smoking, but others may not. Relief
sought from orally ingested marijuana takes much
longer to take effect, and the effect is generally much
stronger than when marijuana is smoked or vaporized.

The difference in the effects of inhaled versus orally
ingested marijuana can be explained by the way the
body processes the drug. While inhaling marijuana
delivers THC directly to the blood stream so that it
moves quickly to the brain and through out the body,
orally ingested marijuana must pass from the stomach
to the small intestine before entering the bloodstream,
which accounts for the longer wait—between an hour
and two hours—for the medical effect. Once absorbed
into the bloodstream, THC must pass through the liver,
where it is broken down into several metabolites, one
of which is 11-hydroxy-THC, a more psycho-actively
potent form of THC. While this same metabolite is
also produced when marijuana is inhaled, the amount
of marijuana needed to be ingested by inhalation is far
less than when taken orally, and is generally not enough
to produce the metabolite at psychoactive levels. It is

the higher levels of 11-hydroxy-THC absorbed by the body when marijuana is orally ingested that causes the effects to last two to three times longer and which produce a dramatically more potent effect.

Because the effect can be much stronger there is an increased risk of experiencing anxiety or panic attacks. For this reason, care should be taken when cooking with marijuana. Patients would do well to begin with small amounts, and increasing according to their comfort level and medication needs.

Vaporization

For those who prefer the quick relief associated with smoked marijuana, as well as the ease of measuring an appropriate dose, vaporization is an effective alternative, which significantly diminishes the amount of toxins delivered into the lungs. This method of using marijuana works by heating it to a temperature hot enough to release the active medical components in marijuana—around 180 degrees Celsius or 356 Fahrenheit—without causing any actual combustion of plant material, which occurs at 230 degrees Celsius and 446 Fahrenheit.

Vaporization allows a patient to achieve all the benefits associated with smoked medical marijuana without the drawbacks of inhaling harmful smoke and toxins. In preliminary studies conducted by Chemic Labs, vaporization of marijuana was shown to produce an inhalable vapor high in THC and cannabinoid content while producing no noticeable level of a wide range of toxins that are usually found in marijuana smoke.

Vaporization is achieved with a device known as a vaporizer. Several companies have vaporizers on the market, each of varying quality. The Volcano® vaporizer, used in the Chemic Labs study, appears to be the most effective—and most expensive—vaporizer on the market as well as being the most expensive.

Obtaining Medical Marijuana

O nce patients have documented their medical conditions and obtained their doctor's approval, or otherwise complied with their state's requirements, how exactly do they obtain their medical marijuana? This problem has plagued the medical marijuana laws from the beginning. The lack of legal avenues for obtaining marijuana continues to be a primary reason given by state legislators for not supporting medical marijuana legislation.

Under federal law the only available supply of marijuana is grown at the University of Mississippi by the National Institute on Drug Abuse (NIDA). They have controlled availability and quality of marijuana for over thirty-six years. This is the marijuana that is used by patients in the Federal Investigational New Drug (IND) Program, and which was used by several states through Therapeutic Research Programs approved by the federal government in the 1980s.

The federal government remains the only source for marijuana under federal law. States and other governmental entities cannot grow marijuana without a permit from the Drug Enforcement Administration (DEA). But the DEA has never allowed any facility except for the University of Mississippi to grow marijuana.

Because states cannot grow marijuana for their own medical programs, and because of the liability associated with providing ill people with confiscated, and possibly contaminated marijuana, the federal government is the only legal source for marijuana under federal law.

Efforts have been made to break up this monopoly. In June 2001, Dr. Lyle Craker, a professor of plant and soil sciences at the University of Massachusetts Amherst, applied to the DEA for a federal research permit to grow marijuana. Craker and other researchers had complained about the poor quality of NIDA's marijuana, claiming that it is not fit or appropriate for research purposes due to abysmally low-potency and the high concentration of non-medically active seeds and stems mixed in the raw materials. Scientists researching medical marijuana have been frustrated by NIDA's record of refusing supplies of marijuana for research purposes, even when research proposals are approved by the FDA. Craker's request was ignored by the DEA for three-and-a-half years. When Craker received no response to his request he filed a lawsuit against the DEA and received a court order compelling the DEA to give a response either granting or denying Prof. Craker's request. The reply finally came. Craker's request was denied. The DEA's denial has been appealed.

While breaking the federal government's monopoly will be a big step forward, it still will not make medical marijuana available for patients. For the foreseeable future, medical marijuana patients in full compliance with their state law will continue to face difficulty in obtaining their medicine.

Buying Medical Marijuana

Even though it is illegal at the state and federal
level to *sell* marijuana, the act of *purchasing* marijuana
Selling pot   is *not* itself defined as a crime. Most drug
is a crime   crimes are broken down into three separate
but buying   offenses: possession, manufacture, and
it is not.   delivery. Generally people who purchase
                 marijuana are guilty of possession as soon
as they are handed the marijuana. Fortunately, patients
who possess marijuana legally under a state's medical
marijuana law are not subject to possession penalties.
Possession is, however, still a *federal* offense.

The sale of marijuana is illegal in all states, even if sold
specifically to and for patients in medical marijuana states.
Contrary to popular belief, sales in California are not legal,
although many cannabis clubs and cooperatives are allowed
to operate, and sell marijuana, at the discretion of local
government (*People ex rel. Lungren v. Peron,* 1997). The DEA,
however, has repeatedly raided cannabis clubs throughout
California to enforce federal law.

Some California counties have begun regulating
cannabis clubs, and limiting the number that may
operate within certain counties. In California, patients
should check with local government to determine
whether a club is approved or not. Patients should
also be aware of the level of permissiveness within
clubs they frequent. If a club is not in the practice of
checking registry cards or appropriate documentation
from a client's doctor before selling marijuana, a
patient should consider finding a new organization.
Many clubs have been, under investigation by
undercover law enforcement—state and federal—looking
to find clubs who will sell marijuana to anyone. While
a legal patient will probably not be prosecuted, it is
always best to stay away from situations that have the
potential to cause problematic and undesirable legal
entanglements.

Possession Limits

Each state has its own limits on how much marijuana a qualified patient is allowed to possess. These limits are all based strictly on quantity, not quality. An ounce of professionally grown Blue Mystic sinsemilla fresh from Northern California is treated just the same as an ounce of ditch weed. With the exception of Washington and California none of the statutory limitations are based on actual medical evidence as to what quantities are medically appropriate or necessary. Rather, the limits are generally based on what was deemed politically acceptable at the time that the state's law was passed.

Under each medical marijuana law, a patient is permitted to possess a quantity of harvested marijuana, *plus* a number of plants. The chart gives a general breakdown of these limits.

A patient who exceeds the law's limits can be criminally prosecuted. In some states, the limits are strictly enforced, while in others they are treated more as guidelines, with some leeway permitted. Some states will prosecute patients for marijuana possessed over the allowed amount, while others may simply confiscate the excess.

In California, the quantities shown in the chart are simply guidelines. Patients are permitted to possess an amount of marijuana sufficient to meet the patient's special medical needs, as determined by the patient's doctor. Individual cities and counties are also given the discretion to officially expand local possession limitations beyond those set by the state. The city of Berkeley passed an ordinance permitting patients to possess up to 10 plants and 2.5 pounds of harvested marijuana. The city of Oakland has an ordinance allowing up to 72 plants with up to 32 square feet of canopy and 2.5 pounds of harvested marijuana.

Possession Limits in Medical Marijuana States

	AK	CA	CO	HI	ME	MT	NV	OR	RI	VT	WA
Leaf & Bud Limits	1 oz	8 oz	2 oz	3 oz	2.5 oz	6 oz	1 oz	24 oz	2.5 oz	2 oz	60 day supply
Plant Limits	6	18	6	7	6	6	7	24	12	3	60 day supply
Mature Plants	3	6	3	3	3	NA	3	6	NA	1	NA
Immature Plants	3	12	3	4	3	NA	4	NA	NA	2	NA
Seedlings	NA	NA	NA	NA	NA	NA	NA	18	NA	NA	NA

In Washington, there is no quantifiable limit or guideline, rather a qualified patient is allowed to possess "a sixty day supply" based on the physician's recommendation (*Washington v. Shepherd*, 2002). This means that what constitutes a "sixty day supply" will vary from patient to patient depending upon their medical need as determined by their physician.

The programs in Nevada and Colorado allow patients to assert a medical necessity defense for violations of the possession limits if the legal limit is inadequate to meet a patient's medical needs. A similar defense was also permitted in Oregon through the end of 2005, but was overturned as the result of a legislative compromise, which significantly increased patient possession limits in exchange for the elimination of this defense.

Each state's possession limits generally apply only to "usable" marijuana, generally defined as the "dried leaves and flowers" of the cannabis plant, and "any mixture or preparation thereof, that are appropriate for medical use." This definition does not include the roots or mature stalks of the plant. Seeds are excluded from this definition in Hawaii, Montana, Oregon, Rhode Island and Vermont, and stems are excluded in Colorado.

Only Maine considers freshly harvested marijuana that has not been dried or cured, and therefore not ready for use, to be usable marijuana. For the remaining states, it's not clear how a freshly harvested plant should be counted. Freshly harvested marijuana is no longer a plant, since it is no longer growing, nor does it become "usable" until it is appropriately cured and prepared for use. Because of this ambiguity, it may be a potential defense for patients who possess usable marijuana up to the possession limit and also have freshly harvested marijuana hanging to dry, to argue that the freshly harvested marijuana should be

excluded from possession limits because it is not yet
usable. This argument makes sense because patients
must have marijuana on hand to medicate during the
curing process, and also because freshly harvested bud
is heavier than marijuana that is fully cured and ready
to smoke.

This defense would be limited by the fact that once
the bud is dried and cured it will be considered usable
marijuana and anything over the allowed possession
limit would then subject the patient to criminal
prosecution. While this may be a viable defense for
possession of excess marijuana during the curing
process, only a court can decide whether it will accept
such an argument.

Quantity Versus Quality

Possession limits are based on quantity, not
quality. What matters is the weight of the marijuana
(or marijuana mixture), not its potency or THC
content. The quantity-not-quality rule is both good
and bad. While this rule is beneficial for patients who
are skilled growers and have access to potent strains
of marijuana, it is restrictive for patients without a
green thumb or access to good quality marijuana,
and who therefore need larger amounts to medicate
due to lower potency marijuana. Two ounces of low-
grade marijuana could disappear very quickly while
two ounces of high-potency marijuana could meet
a patient's medical needs for a substantially longer
period of time.

Conversion to Hashish

A potential solution for unskilled growers may
be found in the art of making hashish, a process that
reduces the weight of marijuana by ninety to ninety-five
percent while retaining all the medically active resins

of the plant material. While patients must remain within the possession limits set by their state program, patients with highly productive, but low-potency, plants may be able to avoid exceeding the limits by turning excess marijuana into hashish. This allows patients to stay within the legal limits and to insure they have an adequate supply of medicine to last them until the next harvest.

While making hash is one way for patients to insure they have sufficient quantities of medicine, the rule limiting marijuana possession by weight has at least one major drawback that patients should be aware of. Because possession is limited by weight and because usable marijuana is typically defined as "any mixture or preparation" of the marijuana plant, any food items made with marijuana can be counted towards a patient's legal limit on the basis of weight. For example, if a patient makes brownies using a quarter ounce of marijuana, the brownies may not count as a quarter ounce of marijuana, but may instead be considered based on the *total weight of the brownies themselves*. While there are no known cases of patients being prosecuted for violating the possession limits due to baking with marijuana, this is a reality of the law that patients should keep in mind.

Patients Helping Patients

Patients often wonder whether it is legal to share medical marijuana with another patient. Both Hawaii and Vermont forbid the transfer of medicine between anyone but a patient and his designated caregiver, but most medical marijuana state laws do not address whether it is legal for patients to share medicine.

Any transfer of marijuana from one individual to another could potentially be considered an illegal delivery regardless of whether money is exchanged or

not. While sale of marijuana is clearly illegal under
state and federal law, it is less clear whether an
exchange of marijuana between
two individuals who may each
legally possess marijuana is also
impermissible under the existing
state programs. Only the state of
Oregon explicitly allows patients
to donate marijuana to other
patients, so long as nothing of
value is given in return.

*Most medical
marijuana
state laws do
not address
the legality of
patients sharing
their medicine.*

Grow Your Own

Most state programs operate on the premise
that patients will grow their own marijuana. This
allows states to take a compassionate stance without
themselves violating federal law, and allows the
opportunity for patients to access medicine the
best way they see fit without the threat of state
prosecution.

While patients in the several medical marijuana
states are generally allowed to grow their own
supply, there still remains the initial problem of
finding seeds or starters. No state with a medical
marijuana program has been able to provide patients
with a legal avenue for obtaining marijuana seeds or
starts. Patients should remember that it is a violation
of federal law to transport marijuana over state or
national borders, and would be well-advised to seek
seeds or starts within their own state to avoid legal
complications associated with transporting marijuana
over state lines.

Generally, states allow a patient to grow six or
seven plants, though there is considerable variation.
Vermont limits patients to three and California's
guidelines allow a patient to grow up to 18 plants, or

more if the patient's doctor says that the patient's special medical needs require more. In most states, the plant limit is divided into two subcategories, "mature" and "immature," which are likewise limited in numbers. A plant that is visibly producing buds or flowers is generally considered a mature plant, while plants that have not begun to flower are considered immature.

The Department of Human Services in the state of Oregon initially defined a mature plant as one where the sex of the plant can be readily determined. However, this rule was problematic because it required patients and police officers to make a determination of plant maturity based on a botanical identification process that many people find difficult. The Oregon law was changed to define "mature plants" as flowering plants that are over a foot in width and height, and creating a new category, "seedlings," which are non-flowering plants under a foot in width and height. It is unclear whether there is still a category of "immature" plant that exists somewhere between the definition of a seedling and a mature plant.

Most states also have restrictions regulating where medical marijuana can be grown. For states with registry programs, patients are generally required to notify the state of the location of their grow site. Most states allow gardens to be grown either indoors or outdoors, but both Rhode Island and Vermont have prohibitions on outdoor grows.

Aside from location, patients should also concern themselves with who has access to their garden, and potential for burglary. Under most state programs, only a patient and designated caregivers may legally have access to marijuana. Patients with kids, roommates, or frequent guests in a building where a garden is kept, should keep their gardens and medicine

in locked rooms or in locked containers. Only the
patient and his caregiver should ever have access to
marijuana, including baked goods and paraphernalia.

Outdoor gardens are more troublesome because
it is harder to limit access solely to a patient and
his caregiver. Locked gates should protect outdoor
gardens and the grower should strive to shield the
garden from public view, e.g., no chain-link fences.
Although outdoor gardens may be legal, patients
who lack discretion will be more likely to draw the
unwelcome attention of law enforcement and burglars.

Outdoor gardens generally work best for patients
who live in rural areas, and who have a higher
expectation of privacy than their urban counterparts.
Patients in urban areas, and those with a lot of foot
traffic in their neighborhoods should strongly consider
keeping their gardens indoors.

Learning How to Grow

For patients learning how to grow, there are
many books available which address techniques for
growing indoors, outdoors, or hydroponically, and
other advanced growing techniques. For patients with
a more hands-on learning style, there may be classes
available through patient advocacy and resource
groups, or other patient based organizations.

Living as a Patient

L ife as a medical marijuana patient is more complex than that of patients treated with standard prescription drugs. The reason is the conflict between federal and state law along with the newness of the medical marijuana programs themselves, which have had little time to correct their kinks. This chapter will cover travel, tenant and employment rights and other lifestyle issues.

There are several limitations on travel that patients and caregivers should be aware of. First, no state permits a patient to operate a motor vehicle while under the influence of marijuana. This is a standard restriction that applies to many prescription drugs as well. Second, several states have limitations on the amount of marijuana that can be transported away from a patient's residence or away from a grow site. Third, travel between states with medical marijuana (even between two medical marijuana states) can subject a patient or caregiver to criminal prosecution.

Driving Under the Influence

Driving under the influence of marijuana is prohibited even in medical marijuana states, yet, most states do not have a mechanism for determining whether a driver is marijuana-impaired. For example, with respect to alcohol intoxication, most states

prohibit driving with a blood alcohol level of .08
or more. As of 2006, Nevada was the only medical
marijuana state to have set such a standard for
marijuana.

In Nevada, an individual is guilty of driving under the
influence of marijuana if a drug test detects levels of
THC in the blood above 2 mg./ml, or in the urine above
10 mg./ml. An individual may also be guilty of driving
under the influence of marijuana if a test detects THC
metabolites with levels in the blood above 5 mg./ml, or
in the urine above mg./ml.

The remaining medical marijuana states have not
set such specific limits with respect to driving with
marijuana in your system. This means that in most
states, the prosecutor must prove that one's driving
was actually impaired as a result of marijuana use.

Zero Tolerance Laws

A handful of state legislatures have passed "zero
tolerance" laws that make it a crime to drive with *any
detectable amount* of marijuana in your system. As of
2006, Rhode Island is the only medical marijuana state
with such a law. There are obvious problems with these
laws because a standard drug test (urinalysis) can often
reveal if the individual has used marijuana in the last
month. This, of course, has nothing to do with whether
the person was actually impaired while driving.

For a medical marijuana user these zero-tolerance
laws can present a serious problem, because the
person will almost always have some detectable
marijuana metabolites in their system. How can a
patient possibly use medical marijuana and live a
normal life, if a zero tolerance state law essentially
threatens to prosecute that person anytime they
get behind the wheel? So, far, the courts have not
answered this question.

Travel Restrictions

Freedom to travel is one of our most basic rights, but medical marijuana patients are likely to encounter more barriers to travel than others. It is specifically a federal crime to transport marijuana across a state border. There are no exemptions here, even if one is traveling from one medical marijuana state to another. This means that patients would have to leave their state without marijuana and acquire a new supply in the state they are visiting to avoid a federal charge of transporting a controlled substance across state lines.

It is a crime to transport marijuana across any state border.

Only the states of Montana and Rhode Island will recognize marijuana registry cards from out of state. This means that medical marijuana patients who are traveling through other states will generally not be protected by those states laws, unless they can assert a medical necessity defense.

Insurance Coverage

If you have medical insurance, visits to your doctor to discuss medical marijuana will be covered. Unfortunately, medical marijuana itself, whether purchased or grown, is not covered by any health insurance companies in the United States. This is a situation that is unlikely to change unless and until marijuana is available through licensed pharmacies.

While the costs of growing and obtaining medical marijuana have yet to be covered by any medical insurance companies, a patient's homeowner's or renter's insurance policy may cover costs associated with stolen or seized marijuana and marijuana plants. Most homeowner's insurance policies contain a clause that covers damage to, or loss of, "trees, shrubs and other plants." Several patients have been successful at

Loss Payments by Insurance

COMPANY	RECIPIENT	LOST	TYPE	PAYMENT	YEAR
All State	Miller	17 plants	Theft	Offered $1,272	1999
CGU Calif.	DeArkland	13 plants	Seized by Police	$6,500	1999
CGU Calif.	Anonymous	3 pounds	Theft	$12,275	2000
Farmers	Jones	14 plants	Theft	$6,850	2000
Nat'l Gen.	Fawcett	Unknown	Seized by Police	$5,525	2001
State Farm	Anonymous	Unknown	Theft	$3,500	1999

Compiled from newspaper accounts, including Maddaus, 2001; Rosenfield, 1999; Sanchez, 2000; and Wilson, 2003.

using this clause in their homeowner's policy to recover some of their financial loss from stolen or seized plants.

The table lists insurance companies that have covered medical marijuana patients whose medicine was stolen or seized by the police.

Policies vary from company to company. Some companies will not cover loss of marijuana by patients at all. Those that do provide coverage differ in the amounts they will pay for the loss of plants and harvested marijuana. Several companies, however, have been surprisingly supportive and practical when dealing with medical marijuana patients.

In an interview with the *San Francisco Examiner*, Diane Tasaka, a spokeswoman for Farmers Insurance Group, stated that under Farmers policy, marijuana "would be covered like any other loss of prescription drug, as long as customers could show proof . . . that they received it under the care of a doctor" (*Rosenfeld*, 1999). A spokesman for State Farm, another homeowner's insurance company, told the *Examiner* that his company doesn't "look at the controversy of the drug as long as it's been sanctioned medically and legally. It's the same as if it were insulin or an expensive antibiotic. It's all brought up as personal property" (*Rosenfeld*, 1999). National General Insurance, however, which paid a $5,525 claim to a medical marijuana patient whose plants were seized and destroyed by the police, was later quoted as stating that it was reconsidering whether to change it's policy to exclude similar future claims (*Maddaus*, 2001).

Family Members

Many medical marijuana states exempt friends and family from any criminal offense that may arise from being in the vicinity of the medical use of marijuana. These states include Hawaii, Montana, Nevada, Rhode Island, Vermont and Washington. Rhode Island even allows friends or family members to administer marijuana to a patient. The Rhode Island exemption, however, appears to be a very limited one. It is unlikely that an individual who is not named as a caregiver can possess, deliver, or assist in the cultivation of marijuana.

Generally, the only people that should have access to marijuana are patients and their designated caregivers. This means that patients or caregivers who live with family or roommates should keep their marijuana locked up, particularly when not on the premises. Spouses, in the states specified above, cannot be prosecuted for being in the kitchen while their partners make marijuana brownies, but they cannot make the brownies themselves, nor should they have access to marijuana when the patient-spouse is away.

Children

The issue of children is somewhat different, although not clearly addressed in any of the medical marijuana programs. The state programs listed above explicitly exempt family members from prosecution for simply being in the presence of the medical use of marijuana, but do not address whether a patient may lawfully medicate in the presence of a child.

Use of illegal drugs has long been a factor considered by states in determining whether to terminate a parent's custodial right to children. Such decisions are made by state governments rather than the federal government. While no state medical marijuana program restricts the state government from considering a patient's medical use of marijuana in termination proceedings, it is highly unlikely that a state will initiate termination proceedings against a medical marijuana patient—absent serious allegations of abuse.

Patients should be aware of particular protocol, however. Most basically, children should not have access to marijuana. Ideally, if patients grow their own marijuana at home, the grow room should be locked and access limited to the patient and his or her caregiver. Usable marijuana, pipes and vaporizers should also be kept out of reach of children, and, preferably, locked up. While this may be inconvenient for the patient, it will help prevent legal or other mishaps with children and teenagers, and stands as evidence of a patient's efforts as a parent to keep their families safe and to abide by the law.

Workplace Issues

Another problem with the existing medical marijuana laws is that they fail to include any employment protections for medical marijuana patients. In fact, most medical marijuana laws expressly state that employers do not need to accommodate the medical use of marijuana in the workplace. This means patients generally have to look elsewhere for employment protection.

Patients have attempted to obtain workplace protections in Oregon, under the Oregon Disabilities Act, and in California, under The Fair Employment and Housing Act. In Oregon, a patient who qualifies as disabled under Oregon's Disabilities Act (ODA) may have a discrimination claim against an employer who fires or hires based upon a patient's medical use of marijuana. Under the ODA, a person is disabled if he "has a physical or mental impairment that substantially limits one or more major life activities, has a record of such an impairment or is regarded as having such an impairment."

In a case called *Washburn v. Columbia Forest Products, Inc.*, however, the Supreme Court of Oregon rejected a patient's discrimination claim under the ODA, finding that he was not disabled and therefore not eligible to bring such a claim. Although the patient fit the definition of disabled under ODA, the state Supreme Court found that he was not disabled because the patient had previously used medications other than marijuana that had alleviated the symptoms of his disability. The court determined that a patient whose condition or symptoms can be alleviated by drugs other than marijuana would not be considered disabled.

It remains possible that Oregon patients who qualify as disabled under ODA, and who have found no treatments other then marijuana that alleviate the symptoms of their disability, will have a viable employment discrimination claim under ODA. Those who are not disabled, or who choose to medicate with marijuana because it has fewer side effects than other equally effective medications, do not presently have any employment protections under Oregon law.

In California in 2006, a court of appeal ruled that the Compassionate Use Act only provides protection from criminal prosecution by the state, and confers no other rights on patients, including those of job protection (*Ross v. Ragingwire Telecommunications*). In addition, the court ruled that under California's Fair Employment and Housing Act, an employer cannot be forced to accommodate an employee by allowing them to engage in behavior that violates federal law. Both of these issues will be reviewed by the California Supreme Court.

On the other side of the spectrum is Vermont, where it is a prosecutable offense to be under the influence of marijuana at the workplace. As of 2006, on Rhode Island offered medical marijuana-using patients explicit employment protections. Hopefully, new medical marijuana laws will more adequately address employment issues, and existing laws will be amended to provide at least some employment protections.

Place Restrictions

Being a legal medical marijuana patient isn't
a license to use marijuana whenever and wherever one
might choose. While each state protects the right of
patients to medicate in their own homes, there are
basic restrictions in each state on where and when a
patient can medicate outside of the home, as well as
where a patient may possess marijuana.

Generally, patients may not medicate in plain view
of the public or in locations that are open to the public.
Only California appears to have some leniency here,
requiring only that patients comply with public smoking
laws. Use of medical marijuana is generally prohibited
in the following areas: public beaches, public parks,
public transportation, public recreation centers, school
grounds, school buses and youth centers. California
prohibits outdoor use of marijuana within 1,000 ft. of a
school, public recreation or youth center, and in Alaska,
use of marijuana within 500 ft. of the same locations is
prohibited.

No state allows the operation of a motor vehicle,
motor boat or aircraft under the influence of marijuana.
Alaska, Colorado, Hawaii and Vermont also prohibit use
of marijuana in any manner that endangers the health
and safety of others.

In two states, a qualified patient is only permitted to
possess marijuana away from a residence or grow site
in certain circumstances. Vermont requires marijuana
possessed in public to be locked in a secure container,
while Alaska requires that marijuana in public be
possessed in a closed container or in a fashion not
visible to the public. In addition, Alaska requires that
marijuana that is transported away from a residence or
grow site be taken directly to another location where it
may lawfully be possessed.

Patient

Rights & Restrictions

As of 2006, Rhode Island was the only state that expressly prohibited a landlord from evicting a tenant, or refusing to lease to a tenant who is a medical marijuana user or caregiver. None of the other medical marijuana states address the issue of tenant rights.

Tenant rights concerning medical marijuana are one of the legal issues that have no clear answers yet. If you are a medical marijuana patient and you own your own home, you are most likely in good shape. Your use of marijuana is lawful and cannot be the basis for taking your house under state forfeiture laws. Unfortunately, there is still the problem of federal forfeiture. Luckily, the federal government usually does not concern itself with growing operations of less than one hundred plants, so you probably have little to worry about.

If you are a medical marijuana user who is also a renter, you are confronted with a number of problems. In most cases, you probably should not tell your landlord that you are a medical marijuana user. First, it's a question of medical privacy. If diabetics have no duty to tell their landlords about their medical problems or medications, neither do you. In fact, because federal law does not recognize the lawfulness of medical marijuana, even in states with medical marijuana laws, there is the remote possibility that you could be prosecuted under federal law and that the federal government could seek forfeiture of the apartment building or house that you are renting. Should this actually happen (which again is a *very* remote possibility), it's probably best that your landlord does not know anything about your medical marijuana use because the landlord may then be able to raise an "innocent owner defense" to the forfeiture action.

A more likely problem for medical marijuana users who rent, is called the "nosey neighbor." This is the person who smells the aroma of marijuana, whether growing or being smoked, and calls the police. As a result, the landlord learns of your medical marijuana use and threatens to evict you because your actions, while legal under state law, are illegal under federal law. Unfortunately, given the federal government's refusal to recognize any legal use of medical marijuana, your landlord has a valid concern, although in practice it is very unlikely that the federal government will seek to take his building.

While you could argue that you are being unlawfully threatened with eviction due to your medical condition, and fight the eviction, doing so could be costly both in terms of legal fees and stress. Right now, this is an area of the law with lots of unanswered questions, which means that the outcome could go either way. Given such an unsteady legal landscape, you may decide to simply move out and find a new place to rent. This, however, presents its own difficulties because the new landlord will likely seek to speak with your old landlord as a reference and learn of your medical marijuana use.

Again, this is one of the big problems with almost all of the medical marijuana laws; they fail to provide for any tenant protections. As a result, until the legislatures or the courts address and define the law in this area, medical marijuana users are left in limbo.

Return of Seized Marijuana

When a police officer initially confronts someone for possessing or growing marijuana, the officer usually does not know whether the person is a qualified patient. Unless the person is registered, or is otherwise able to convince the officer that he or she is a legal medical user, it's routine for the officer to arrest or cite the person, seize any marijuana, and let the courts sort it out. Obviously, such circumstances will cause a lot of stress for the patients involved. It can also result in the loss of expensive and much needed medicine.

Fortunately, most medical marijuana states require the return of the property undamaged once a patient's status has been verified or once the District Attorney (DA) has decided that no prosecutable offense has taken place. Oregon's law makes this very explicit, stating that if police officers seize a patient's marijuana the marijuana "shall not be harmed, neglected, injured or destroyed" by law enforcement, the marijuana may not be forfeited, and usable marijuana must be returned immediately upon a determination that it was medical marijuana. Unfortunately, the provision requiring protection of the property excludes plants, noting, "A law enforcement agency has no responsibility to maintain live marijuana plants lawfully seized." If the DA decides to prosecute, the patient must be acquitted of wrongdoing for the property to be returned. Generally, medical marijuana and related property can only be permanently seized after a criminal conviction.

This provision of the state programs has been exercised successfully by patients in both the states of Oregon and Colorado. A patient in Portland, Oregon, requested the return of marijuana that had been seized by the Portland police, after his legal status had been verified. The City of Portland argued that to return the marijuana would violate the federal prohibition on delivery of controlled substances. An Oregon Appellate Court found that Portland police had no excuse for refusing to return marijuana to a patient against whom charges had been dismissed, as required by the Oregon Medical Marijuana Act, and pointed out that federal law grants immunity to local law enforcement for the "enforcement of any law or municipal ordinance relating to controlled substances," and that this would include protection for the return of marijuana under state law (*Oregon v. Kama*, 2002).

Like Oregon, Colorado requires police officers to safeguard any seized medical marijuana or related property while awaiting resolution of a case. Unlike, Oregon, Colorado's law does not explicitly exclude plants from this requirement. Rather, in clear language (especially when compared to Oregon's similar provision) Colorado's law states: "Any property interest that is possessed, owned, or used in connection with the medical use of marijuana or acts incidental to such use, shall not be harmed, neglected, injured, or destroyed while in the possession of state or local law enforcement officials where such property has been seized in connection with the claimed medical use of marijuana."

Nevertheless, even in a state with such a provision, it can often take considerable effort to get the police to live up to the law. Thomas Lawrence, a medical marijuana patient in Colorado, had his marijuana seized during a traffic stop when he failed to produce a registry identification card. After a month and a half of

wrangling with law enforcement, including verification
of Lawrence's legal status and a court order demanding
the return of Lawrence's medicine, the police
reluctantly returned the confiscated marijuana.

This sort of wrangling is common in medical
marijuana cases when patients seek the return of their
medicine after winning their case. Even in California,
the courts are split. Some judges routinely order
confiscated marijuana returned to people who prove
they are lawful medical marijuana patients, while other
judges actually refuse to do so, arguing that they
have no legal authority to return marijuana, or that
the federal Controlled Substances Act prevents the
court from returning (i.e., "distributing") marijuana to
a patient. This is a bogus argument. A provision of
federal law states that criminal liability shall not be
imposed under the Controlled Substances Act upon
any law enforcement officer who is lawfully engaged
in the enforcement of state laws relating to controlled
substances. California's medical marijuana law (like
the other state marijuana laws) is clearly a state law
relating to controlled substances.

In every case, qualified patients who have their
marijuana seized should file a motion for return of the
property. The patient has nothing to lose, and it's
important for medical marijuana patients to assert
the same rights that other patients are afforded. A
diabetic who had his or her insulin and syringes
seized would expect to have them returned, and
police departments, prosecutors, and courts, need to
recognize that medical marijuana patients are entitled
to the very same right.

While the majority of medical marijuana states
provide for the return of lawfully possessed
marijuana, the state of Vermont explicitly excuses law
enforcement from returning marijuana or paraphernalia,
even after a patient's legal status has been verified.

Penalties

As might be expected, there are penalties in most states for individuals who violate the medical marijuana law. Generally, if certain activities are not protected by a medical marijuana program and are prohibited under state law, the individual will be charged with violating state law.

Violations of medical marijuana laws may result in the revocation of a patient's legal status in many states, including Alaska, Colorado, Nevada or Oregon. A patient may be excluded from reapplying to the program for one year in Alaska and Colorado, and six months in Nevada and Oregon. In addition, violation of Oregon's medical marijuana law may result in the patient forfeiting *all* protections of the program. For example, if a patient is driving under the influence of marijuana while transporting several ounces from a grow site to his residence, the patient can be charged with driving under the influence as well as possession of a controlled substance.

The remaining medical marijuana states carry no specific penalties, aside from enforcement of state law, for violations of their medical marijuana program. Although several states have specific fraud offenses related to their medical marijuana laws.

Physician Rights & Responsibilities

The role of physicians is vital to the functioning of state medical marijuana programs. In each state program, a patient's right to use marijuana is contingent upon having a physician's approval or recommendation. Exactly what a physician must do or provide varies from state to state, with some state programs requiring a recommendation and others requiring mere acknowledgment that the use of marijuana may be beneficial in the treatment of a patient's condition.

Because of the significant role played by physicians in the functioning of the state programs, physicians have been targets of the federal government and state medical boards interested in shutting down these state programs. This chapter will explore the various campaigns that have been leveled against physicians in an attempt to shut down the medical marijuana programs, and provide guidelines that physicians should observe when recommending the medical use of marijuana to patients.

Right to Discuss Medical Marijuana

The first attack on physicians came in 1996 after the federal government issued a decree immediately following the passage of medical marijuana initiatives in California and Arizona. The policy, titled "The Administration's Response to the Passage of California Proposition 215 and Arizona Proposition 200" was announced by Barry McCaffrey, then Director of the Office of National Drug Control Policy (ONDCP), on December 30, 1996. This policy declared that physicians who recommended or prescribed medical marijuana risk revocation of their DEA license to prescribe controlled substances.

With physicians fearing loss of their right to prescribe if they recommended or approved of a patient's use of marijuana, California's Compassionate Use Act would have been effectively dead. But, a coalition of doctors and patients filed an action to prevent the federal government from enforcing the policy.

The federal Court of Appeal for the Ninth Circuit, ruled in favor of the doctors, finding that the federal policy impermissibly infringed on the freedom of speech rights of both physicians and patients (*Conant v. Walters*, 2001). The First Amendment, said the court, protects a physician who discusses the risks and benefits of using marijuana medicinally with a patient, and who ultimately recommends such use. As a result, none of these actions can subject a physician to criminal liability. In addition, a medical board is prohibited from taking administrative action or initiating an investigation into a physician's practice based *solely* on a recommendation for the medical use of marijuana.

There are two things the decision does *not* do. First, marijuana is a Schedule I substance under federal law, and hence cannot be prescribed. The decision in the *Conant* case does not change this: a doctor has no First Amendment right to write a patient a prescription for marijuana. The protection extends only to discussing, recommending, or approving of a patient's use of medical marijuana.

Second, the *Conant* decision does not insulate a physician from using speech or actions to assist a patient in actually *acquiring* marijuana. The government remains free to prosecute any physician who aids or abets a patient in growing or obtaining marijuana, or who joins in a conspiracy with a patient. In order to charge a doctor with aiding and abetting or conspiracy, the government must have "substantial evidence" that the doctor and patient actively worked together or entered an agreement to acquire or grow marijuana.

There has been one case where the federal government felt it had substantial evidence of such a conspiracy. In 2005, Dr. Marian "Mollie" Fry and her husband, attorney Dale Schafer, were indicted on federal charges of conspiracy to distribute marijuana, conspiracy to manufacture marijuana and conspiracy to grow 100 or more plants. The doctor/attorney duo operated the California Medical Research Center, where they offered patients both medical and legal consultations. Dale Schafer acted as a caregiver for his wife, a cancer patient, as well as some of his wife's patients who received recommendations through the Center. As of 2006, this case had not gone to trial, and neither Dr. Fry nor attorney Schafer have been convicted of any charges.* This case underscores that physicians, who venture outside of simply providing exams and recommendations may draw the attention of federal or state officials and potentially subject themselves (and their patients) to conspiracy charges.

*See www.docfry.com for updates in this case.

The Ninth Circuit's decision in *Conant* was appealed to the United States Supreme Court by the Bush Administration, but the Supreme Court refused to review the case. As a result, the Ninth Circuit's decision in *Conant* is in full force and effect in all the states covered by the Ninth Circuit: California, Oregon, Washington, Arizona, Montana, Idaho, Nevada, Alaska, Hawaii, (and the unincorporated territories, Guam and the Northern Mariana Islands). While areas outside the Ninth Circuit's jurisdiction are not required to follow the decision in *Conant*, the government will have an uphill battle convincing a court not to follow the reasoning in *Conant*. Thus as a practical matter, the First Amendment protects the right of physicians to discuss marijuana with their patients anywhere in the U.S. This includes those states that do *not* (yet) have medical marijuana laws.

State Medical Board Actions

While physicians are fairly well protected from state or federal criminal prosecution for discussing medical marijuana with patients, the Medical Boards of California and Oregon have both investigated and levied sanctions against doctors known for their willingness to recommend the medical use of marijuana. While sanctioning by a state medical board is more probable than criminal prosecution, conscientious physicians should have little to worry about. The circumstances surrounding the investigations of physicians known to have come under the scrutiny of various state medical boards are explored below.

Failing to Conduct Exams and Keep Medical Records

Dr. Leveque is an 80-year-old Osteopathic physician in Oregon with a history of trouble with the state's Medical Board. In 1981 and 1984, following Board investigations, Leveque agreed to stop prescribing drugs to patients. In 1986, Leveque came under investigation for improper treatment of pain, and was later placed on ten years probation, ordered to close his practice, and barred from prescribing drugs. This was long before Oregon enacted its medical marijuana law in 1998.

The Board took notice of Dr. Leveque again in July of 2001, when it learned that he had signed forty percent of Oregon's then 2,227 registered medical marijuana patients. Upon investigation, the Board concluded that Dr. Leveque had not conducted physical exams or maintained medical records on many of these patients. This prompted the Board to issue a new rule requiring that an attending physician provide these services before qualifying patients for the state medical marijuana program. This rule was applied retroactively by the Board, which forced hundreds of pending applicants signed by Dr. Leveque to sign releases allowing state officials to inspect their medical charts before the applications could be processed.

On January 17, 2002, the state's Medical Board charged Dr. Leveque with unprofessional conduct in his approval of over 1,000 patients for the state's medical marijuana program. In the complaint, the Board claimed that Dr. Leveque approved patients for the program without "examining the patient, conducting medical tests, maintaining an adequate medical chart, reviewing possible contra indications or conferring with other medical care providers" (Christie, 2002). The Board cited three examples demonstrating

Dr. Leveque's failure to meet the standard of care Oregon doctors are required to meet, with two of the examples involving patients Dr. Leveque approved for the state program without ever having met or examined in person.

In May 2002, the Board suspended Dr. Leveque's medical license for ninety days, placed him on probation for ten years and fined him $5,000. In addition, the Board ordered Dr. Leveque to undergo physical and psychological examinations to determine his competency to practice medicine, and to report to the Board in person at each of its quarterly meetings. Dr. Leveque protested that Oregon's medical marijuana statute bars the Board from disciplining doctors who recommend marijuana, but the Board insisted that sanctions were not based on his marijuana recommendations but rather on his failure to meet the standards of care required of Oregon physicians.

In November 2003, Dr. Leveque came under investigation again following allegations that his physical examination of patients was too cursory. As a result, his license was suspended a second time in March, 2004. On October 15, 2004, the Board issued a final order revoking Dr. Leveque's license to practice medicine. In the revocation order, the Board explained that "with no effort expended to confirm a patient's complaint with a tailored evaluation... [Leveque] relied on his patients' statements that using marijuana provided them better relief from pain and other debilitating conditions than the use of other pharmaceuticals," The Board concluded that Dr. Leveque's "continued practice of medicine constitutes an immediate danger to the health and safety of the public" (*Gardner*, 2004). As of 2006, Dr. Leveque is the only physician in the United States to have had his license to practice medicine revoked for improperly recommending marijuana for medical use.

While the high number of medical marijuana
recommendations by Dr. Leveque most certainly played
a role in the Board levying sanctions against him, and
ultimately revoking his license to practice, a physician
should be able to avoid such circumstances by
following reasonable medical standards and practices.
Most essential appears to be meeting the patients in
person, conducting a thorough medical history and
physical examination, and properly maintaining medical
records.

California's Compassionate Use Act

As of 2006, at least a dozen physicians have been
investigated and/or sanctioned by the Medical Board
of California. Taken together these doctors have
recommended the medical use of marijuana to nearly
50,000 patients. No doubt this explains some of
the interest the Medical Board has taken in these
physicians. There are several other explanations for
the high level of scrutiny being applied in California
that are worth exploring. One is the flexibility given to
physicians under the state's Compassionate Use Act,
and the other surrounds the politics and history of
the California Attorney General's office. It must also
be remembered that California's medical marijuana
program being the oldest of the state programs, is
the major testing ground of the legal boundaries to
these programs. These factors also contribute to the
relatively high number of investigations in that state.

Unlike other state programs, which have a list of
qualifying medical conditions that are legally treatable
by marijuana, California's Compassionate Use Act is
more open-ended. When drafting Prop. 215, in addition
to a list of qualifying medical conditions, a clause
was included at the urging of Dr. Tod Mikuriya, one

of the physicians discussed below, to allow the use of marijuana for "any other illness for which marijuana provides relief."

This clause gives a physician flexibility in deciding what particular medical conditions may appropriately be treated with marijuana, flexibility that has made the Medical Board of California nervous. When a state law lists only a finite number of conditions eligible for treatment with marijuana it is relatively easy to determine whether a physician is operating within the scope of the law. Without such a closed set of conditions it becomes less and less clear to medical boards upon what standards physicians have based their medical marijuana recommendations.

California's Compassionate Use Act was supplemented in 2003 by Senate Bill 420. The amended language limits the scope of that catchall phrase. Under the new language, physicians are limited to recommending marijuana to treat chronic or persistent medical conditions that either: (1) substantially limit the ability of the person to conduct one or more major life activities (as defined in the Americans with Disabilities Act of 1990) or (2) if left unalleviated, may cause serious harm to the patient's safety or physical or mental health. While this new language qualifies and limits what was originally allowed under the Compassionate Use Act, physicians still retain a significant amount of flexibility, flexibility which is generally unseen in other state programs.

Another important reason for the number of medical board investigations in California may be attributed to former California Attorney General Dan Lungren, who was in office when Californian voters approved medical marijuana at the ballot in 1996. From the beginning, Lungren opposed medical marijuana. Rather than work to enforce state law, as was his duty, Lungren abandoned the people of California and saddled up with Barry McCaffrey, the then federal "Drug Czar." The two strategized on how to defeat the new law, and advised local law enforcement and prosecutors to continue arresting and prosecuting individuals who possessed or cultivated marijuana for medical purposes.

In 1997, Lungren's Senior Deputy, John Gordnier, sent a memo to the local district attorneys offices in each of California's fifty-eight counties, requesting notification of any cases involving medical marijuana recommendations by Dr. Tod Mikuriya and Dr. Eugene Schoenfeld (*Gardner*, 2003A). Most if not every single one of the subsequent complaints to the Medical Board about Dr. Mikuriya came not from patients but from prosecutor's who failed to get convictions against patients with medical marijuana approvals from Dr. Mikuriya.

Too Many Patient Recommendations

Dr. Tod Mikuriya spent much of his career researching marijuana's medicinal benefits, starting in 1967 when he was recruited by the National Institute of Mental Health to act as the consulting psychiatrist on marijuana research. Since that time, Dr. Mikuriya has written numerous articles on the effects and benefits of marijuana, as well as coauthoring the *Marijuana Medical Handbook: A Guide to Therapeutic Use*. He was also a coauthor and medical advisor to the team that drafted California's Compassionate Use Act.

When the Compassionate Use Act passed in 1996, Dr. Mikuriya shifted the focus of his medical practice to medical marijuana, becoming a specialist in the area. Since that time, he has recommended marijuana to more than ten thousand patients.

Dr. Mikuriya's problems began immediately after the passage of the Act. On December 30, 1996, just two months after voters approved the Act, Dr. Mikuriya was publicly accused by Drug Czar Barry McCaffrey of promoting "Cheech and Chong medicine." He was also placed on the watch-list of law enforcement and prosecutors around the state, at the request of California Attorney General Dan Lungren. Prosecutors, who lost marijuana cases in court when the defendant presented a medical recommendation from Dr. Mikuriya, began forwarding information to the Medical Board, prompting an investigation into Dr. Mikuriya's medical practice. In 2002, over the objections of Dr. Mikuriya and his patients, the Medical Board subpoenaed the private medical records for forty-seven of his patients, and commenced investigation into seventeen of those files.

Based on the Board's investigation, Dr. Mikuriya was charged with "unprofessional conduct" and "gross negligence," for his alleged failure to keep adequate records, conduct proper and complete examinations, and for failing to follow-up with patients. Mikuriya filed a motion to dismiss the charges, citing the "absolute immunity" conferred upon doctors who recommend marijuana under the Compassionate Use Act, which states that "no physician in this state shall be punished, or denied any right or privilege, for having recommended marijuana to a patient for medical purposes."

On August 4, 2003, Administrative Law Judge Jonathan Lew rejected Mikuriya's motion to dismiss. In his opinion, Judge Lew stated:

> It is presumed that physicians who recommend marijuana under the Act will follow accepted medical practice standards and make good faith recommendations based on honest medical judgments. Complainant [The Attorney General, on behalf of the

Medical Board] correctly notes that to hold otherwise
and to extend absolute immunity to physicians would
allow them to simply issue recommendations without
the exercise of sound medical judgment and with no
oversight" (Gardner, 2003B).

The Medical Board offered Dr. Mikuriya a deal which
would have placed him on four years probation,
required him to take an ethics course and a clinical
training program, and reimburse the Board $10,000 for
investigation costs. Dr. Mikuriya rejected the offer,
leaving open the possibility that the Medical Board
would revoke his license.

During a subsequent hearing, which commenced
on September 3, 2003, the prosecution called two
witnesses to make its case. The first witness was a
Kaiser psychiatrist by the name of Dr. Laura Duskin,
who reviewed the files of seventeen patients who
allegedly received substandard care from Dr. Mikuriya.
Dr. Duskin presented her opinion that Dr. Mikuriya was
grossly negligent in all seventeen cases, because his
examinations were so superficial.

None of the 17 named patients filed complaints
with the Board, nor were they even interviewed by Dr.
Duskin to determine the extent of their examinations.
In fact, nine of the seventeen patients came to the
hearing and testified that Dr. Mikuriya was thorough
and attentive during their medical examinations, and
each expressed gratitude for Mikuriya's assistance and
care.

An undercover narcotics agent named Steve Gossett
also testified. Gossett testified that Dr. Mikuriya
gave him a marijuana recommendation after Gossett
fraudulently represented himself as a victim of chronic
shoulder pain.

On April 19, 2004, Judge Jonathan Lew found that Dr. Mikuriya had failed to properly examine his patients before recommending marijuana, and placed him on five years probation, during which time his practice and medical record-keeping would be monitored by another physician. Lew also imposed a fine of $75,000 to help pay for investigation-related expenses of the Board. Mikuriya appealed this decision to the Superior Court, and lost on Feb. 10, 2006. Mikuriya may still appeal the decision to the California Court of Appeals.

Weakness in the Policy

The 1997 policy promulgated by the California Medical Board, which was pivotal in the investigation of Mikuriya, is merely an advisory policy and not an official regulation. The policy does not define a standard of medical practice for physicians who evaluate medical marijuana patients, an omission that Dr. Mikuriya has long criticized. In March 2003, Dr. Mikuriya and Frank Lucido, MD, submitted a draft proposal of "minimum practice standards" to be used with medical marijuana patients, for approval by the California Medical Association (CMA). The CMA adopted a modified version of the proposal, and agreed to work with the Medical Board to revise the 1997 policy statement. After working on a joint task force with the CMA, the California Medical Board adopted a new policy statement* on May 7, 2004, which provides that:

> ... the mere receipt of a complaint that [a physician is recommending medical marijuana will not generate an investigation absent additional information indicating that the physician is not adhering to accepted medical standards.

It is not clear whether Dr. Mikuriya would have been disciplined under the new standard.

*For full text, see: www.medbd.ca.gov/Medical_Marijuana.htm.

Recommending Medical Marijuana for a Minor

Dr. Mike Alcalay came under investigation after recommending the medical use of marijuana for an eight year old boy who was about to be removed from his family to a residential treatment center to treat uncontrollable violent and aggressive behavior. Dr. Alcalay, who never met the boy in person, based his recommendation on a review of the boy's medical records as well as extensive phone conversations with the boy's mother. The Board subpoenaed Dr. Alcalay's patient medical records and requested that he submit to a "voluntary interview," which he agreed to. After investigation, the complaint against Alcalay was dismissed in May of 2003.

A book titled *Jeffrey's Journey*, about the eight year old boy who was treated by Dr. Alcalay was subsequently published. The authors, who are the boy's mother and grandmother, recount the various attempts at treating Jeffrey's violent rages and the successful experiences the family had while treating him with marijuana.

Dr. Frank Lucido was also investigated for recommending marijuana to a minor. The complaint against Dr. Lucido came from a high school administrator after a teenage patient was found in possession of marijuana while at school. Possession of medical marijuana at a school is expressly prohibited under California's Compassionate Use Act.

Dr. Lucido had met his patient in person and recommended marijuana to treat his hyperactivity disorder after other medications, including Ritalin, Lithium and Prozac, failed to produce results or caused unacceptable side effects. After commencing treatment with medical marijuana the minor achieved excellent grades and was able to hold down a part-time job.

The Board subpoenaed Dr. Lucido's patient medical records and also requested that he submit to a "voluntary interview," which he declined. In July, 2003, the Board decided not to take any action against Dr. Lucido, instead forwarding his case to the Attorney General's office for possible prosecution. The Attorney General's office decided not to pursue the case against Dr. Lucido.

In response to the Medical Board's actions against him and other California physicians Dr. Lucido announced that he would be "monitoring all cases that come to my attention of doctors being investigated for having recommended cannabis."

Protecting Patient Privacy

The California Board of Medical Examiners had routinely subpoenaed patient medical records from doctors who recommended medical marijuana to patients, a practice that went unchallenged until a complaint was lodged against Dr. David Bearman. The complaint against Dr. Bearman came from a state park ranger whose attempt to confiscate marijuana from a camper was frustrated by a letter approving of the individual's medical use of marijuana, signed by the doctor. The Medical Board subpoenaed the patient's files, but Bearman refused to provide them, citing doctor-patient confidentiality. After two years of legal wrangling, Bearman's refusal to supply the records was eventually upheld by the California Court of Appeal for the Second District. The court ruled that the Medical Board cannot "delve into an area of reasonably expected privacy simply because it wants assurance the law is not violated or a doctor is not negligent in treatment of his or her patient" (*Bearman v. Superior Court*, 2004).

Target of Undercover Investigation

The California Board of Medical Examiners suspended Dr. William Eidelman's license to practice in May 2002 for recommending the medical use of marijuana without proper medical cause. The suspension was based on Eidelman's approval of medical marijuana for use by four separate undercover police officers. Dr. Eidelman was later placed on five years probation by the Board (*Gardner*, 2003C).

Advertising

Dr. Stephen Ellis came under investigation after the Medical Board took notice of advertisements placed by Ellis in several newspapers advertising his willingness to write medical marijuana recommendations. No complaints were lodged against Dr. Ellis by patients or by others. The inquiry into Ellis' practice was eventually closed (*Gardner*, 2003C).

Conclusion

Nearly all of the physicians who have been investigated by state medical boards have made medical marijuana referrals a significant portion of their medical practice and in many cases have provided medical marijuana recommendations to a thousand patients or more. The likelihood of physicians being investigated for a handful of recommendations, or even several hundred, appears doubtful.

When physicians are investigated for recommending marijuana to patients they are generally held to a much higher standard of care than is usually required in similar circumstances. This is unfair, but it's the unfortunate reality. Physicians can probably avoid investigations and sanctions for recommending the medical use of marijuana by conducting thorough exams, heavily documenting their files, and providing the same standard of care as when they prescribe other medications to patients.

Dealing with Cops

Much of what's known as "constitutional law" focuses on the rights of people who are confronted by police officers. This is a complex area of the law and constantly evolving. With that in mind, there are five fundamental legal rules that a medical marijuana patient must understand if ever confronted by a police officer. For an entire book on this topic, see Richard Glen Boire's book *Marijuana Law*.

Not Immune From Arrest

Being a qualified medical marijuana patient or caregiver provides a huge amount of comfort, and a welcome relief from constant fears of being sent to prison, but it's important, however, to never forget that it is *not a complete immunization from being arrested or even convicted for a marijuana offense.* Even a legitimate patient or caregiver can be arrested if a police officer has reason to believe that the person is exceeding any aspect of the state's medical marijuana law, or if the police officer is unable to confirm the person's status.

Accordingly, it's wise not to treat your patient or caregiver status as a badge to flaunt your use or cultivation of marijuana. Doing so is likely to attract unnecessary and unwelcome law enforcement attention. This is never a good thing. It can lead to an arrest for marijuana or other charges, and even if you end up winning your case in court, it can be expensive and stressful. Keep a low profile.

Maintain a Low Profile

Key to staying out of the eyes and arms of big brother, is keeping your medical marijuana under wraps. This should be common sense, but it's also very important for upholding your constitutional rights. The Fourth Amendment only protects you from "unreasonable" searches and seizures. The courts have made very clear, that it's perfectly reasonable (with only a few exceptions) for a police officer to seize marijuana without a warrant anytime an officer sees it in plain view. It's true that you might get it back *if* the officer finds that you're an authorized patient or caregiver, but why take that chance, and why invite an unnecessary encounter with a cop?

The Fourth Amendment's protection against unreasonable searches and seizures is one of our most powerful rights as free people. By putting marijuana or marijuana paraphernalia in plan view, you are waiving this powerful protection and giving a police officer a free pass to search you and hassle you. Don't do it!

Never Consent to a Warrantless Search

The vast majority of marijuana-related arrests result from *warrantless* searches. It's absolutely astounding how many people get arrested only because they consent to a search and the officer finds some marijuana. Evidently these people do not understand that they have a constitutional right to refuse to consent. In most cases, without even knowing it, people relinquish a substantial portion of their Fourth

Amendment rights by consenting to an officer's request to search. You should never hesitate to assert your constitutional rights, particularly when they are all that stand between freedom and arrest on a marijuana charge.

The sad fact is that most people believe that they are under some kind of obligation to acquiesce when an officer contacts them and asks permission to search them or their belongings. The truth is the exact opposite—you *Anything you* have a right to associate with, and *say will be used* speak to, whomever you please. *against you.* In this respect, there is nothing special about a police officer. Assuming you would not let a complete stranger look through your purse or search your pockets, why would you allow a police officer to do so—especially if you knew you were in possession of marijuana?"

Generally speaking, a person gains nothing by consenting to a police officer's request to conduct a warrantless search. The many court cases on the subject reveal the great danger that often accompanies the waiver of the constitutional right to remain free from such searches. Just remember, *any officer who asks your permission to search is looking for evidence that he doesn't have—yet.* The whole point of a search is to look for incriminating evidence! Little is to be gained and much can be lost by waiving a constitutional right.

If an officer hassles you when you refuse to consent to a search, just tell him that you have personal items and you object to his violating your constitutional right to privacy. If the officer still proceeds to search you and finds marijuana, your attorney can argue that the marijuana was discovered through an illegal search and hence should be thrown out of court.

Don't Talk to Cops

Police officers gather much of their incriminating information just by talking to people. Often, an officer will have a "hunch" that a person is "up to something," and hope that by talking to the person he might detect some concrete evidence of a crime, such as possession of marijuana. This commonly occurs in airports when drug-enforcement agents think a person may be transporting drugs, but have no real evidence. In such situations, the agents will often contact the person and inform him that they are conducting a narcotics investigation and would like to talk to him. In such a pressure-packed situation, many people (often those who actually *are* carrying drugs) foolishly agree to speak with the agents, perhaps believing that it would be more suspicious to decline to speak. These conversations often give the agent additional evidence that the person is in possession of drugs, leading to the person's arrest. In addition, if the person is prosecuted, any statements he made during the contact will be used against him.

Therefore, generally speaking, the cases teach that people who use marijuana should be on their guard whenever approached by a police officer interested in engaging in small talk. Numerous arrests make abundantly clear that, in the event of a contact, a person in possession of marijuana is usually well-advised to tell the officer that he or she is late for an appointment and then continue on his or her way. Unless the officer has a specific reason to believe the person is involved in criminal activity, he must respect the person's wishes and allow him or her to leave."

There is one important exception. If it is crystal clear that an officer has sufficient evidence to arrest you on the spot for a marijuana offense, then by all means assert your qualified patient or caregiver status. Anytime you are in possession of marijuana it is vital that you carry with you proof of your qualified patient or caretaker status. In registry states, this means having a copy of your registration card with you at all times. In nonregistry states, patients should carry copies of their medical records or other documentary proof of a doctor's recommendation.

Create a Patient/Caretaker ID Card

Carrying around medical documents is not always practical. As a result, patients in nonregistry states should consider making their own unofficial wallet cards. The card should state, "I am an authorized medical marijuana patient pursuant to [insert your state's medical marijuana law—see Appendix for official names of the state statutes]. Then include your name as well as the recommending physician's name, office address, and all phone numbers. Such a card can be made on a home computer and then laminated at a copy shop.

Carry the card in your wallet at all times—just like your driver's license or state ID card. If detained by an enforcement officer and the officer becomes aware of your medicine, take out your card and read directly from it. While the card is not "official," it contains the information that an officer can use to verify your lawful status as a patient or caretaker qualified to possess medical marijuana. Additionally, the fact that the card looks "official" and is laminated gives an air of legality and shows that you are serious and prepared.

In the event of an arrest, the card can serve as documentary proof that you informed the officer of your patient status at the time of arrest—an act that places the officer on notice not to destroy your medicine.

There's no need to spill your guts when asserting your rights. Having a prepared card such as described

above reminds you to not say too much. All you
need to state is that you are a qualified patient or
caregiver under your state's law. If you have an actual
registration card make sure to show it to the officer.

Do not elaborate. Do not talk about the specifics of
your medical condition. Do not talk about how much
marijuana you use or grow. Do not consent to any
searches. Do not invite the officer into your house. Just
assert your medical authorization and provide your
registration card or other proof of your status.

Remain Silent and Demand an Attorney

In the event that you are arrested, do not talk
with the police. At this point they are only looking for
more evidence to use against you, and by speaking
with them you are handing them evidence on a silver
platter. As noted above, just assert your medical status,
but otherwise remain silent and demand a lawyer.
Just repeat: "I am a lawful medical marijuana patient
[or caregiver] under state law. I refuse to answer any
questions, as is my right under the Fifth Amendment.
I request an attorney, as is my right under the Sixth
Amendment."

Medical Marijuana Statutes

Below is a list of the primary medical marijuana laws for readers who would like to look up the exact provisions of a particular state's law. We suggest that readers do so by visiting the free legal research site www.findlaw.com, clicking on the state of interest, and then performing a search for the sections listed below. This is not an exhaustive list of the medical marijuana laws, but rather a listing of the primary code section for each state's medical marijuana law. In most cases, however, referencing the sections below will link to other related code sections.

Remember, the laws are constantly changing and new court cases can change how they are interpreted. For that reason, it is always wise to consult an attorney after educating yourself.

Alaska

Alaska Statutes, section 17.37 (2005).

California

California Health & Safety Code, section 11362.5 et. seq. (2004).

Colorado

Colo. Const. Art. XVIII, Section 14 (2005).

Hawaii

Hawaii Revised Statutes, section 329-121 (2004).

Maine

Maine Revised Statutes, Tit. 22, section 2383-B (2004).

Montana

Montana Codes Annotated, section 50-46-101 (2004).

Nevada

Nevada Revised Statutes, section 453A (2004).

Oregon

Oregon Revised Statutes, section 475.300 (2005).

Rhode Island

General Laws of Rhode Island, section 21-28.6 (2005).

Vermont

Vermont Statutes Annotated, Tit. 18, section 4471 (2004).

Washington

Revised Code of Washington, section 69.51A (2003).

Resources

The following resources include government agencies in charge of implementing medical marijuana registry programs, and non-governmental organizations that provide clinics and assistance to medical marijuana patients and others seeking to qualify as medical marijuana patients. This list is not exhaustive, but may provide some initial direction to those who feel they may benefit from medical marijuana.

Alaska

Alaska Dept. of Health and Social Services
Marijuana Registry
Attention: Terry Ahrens
P.O. Box 110699
Juneau, Alaska 99811-0699
Phone: 907-465-5423
Email: terry_ahrens@health.state.ak.us

California

California Dept. of Health Services
Office of County Health Services
Attention: Medical Marijuana Program
MS 5203, PO Box 997413
Sacramento, California 95899-7413
Email: mmpinfor@dhs.ca.gov
www.dhs.ca.gov/mmp/

Due to the high number of dispensaries, cooperatives and buyers clubs in California, and due to the sometimes, erratic or short-lived existence of many of these organizations, it is impractical to make a comprehensive list here. The following organizations should be consulted for more information:

Americans for Safe Access
1322 Webster Street, Suite 208
Oakland, California 94612
Phone: 510-251-1856 Toll-Free: 888-929-4367
Fax: 510-251-2036
Email: info@safeaccessnow.org
www.safeaccessnow.org

California NORML
2215-R Market Street #278
San Francisco, California 94144
Phone: 415-563-5858
www.canorml.org

Colorado

Medical Marijuana Registry
Colorado Depart Public Health and Environment
HSVR-ADM2-A1
4300 Cherry Creek Drive South
Denver, Colorado 80246-1530
Phone: 303-692-2184
Email: medical.marijuana@state.co.us
www.cdphe.state.co.us/hs/medicalmarijuana/
marijuanafactsheet.asp

Sensible Colorado
P.O. Box 18768
Denver, Colorado 80218-0768
Phone: 720-890-4247
Email: info@sensiblecolorado.org
www.sensiblecolorado.org

The Hemp & Cannabis Foundation Medical Clinic
Toll Free: 1-800-723-0188
www.thc-foundation.org/

Hawaii

Hawaii Dept. of Public Safety
919 Ala Moana Boulevard
Honolulu, Hawaii 96814
Phone: 808-594-0150

Dr. Robert Ley & Dr. Burton Feinerman
Kukui Mall #D-101
1819 S. Kihei Rd
Kihei, Hawaii 96753
Phone: 808-874-5141
www.mjmaui.com/

Patients Without Time (Maui)
71 Baldwin Avenue
Suite C-3
Paia, Hawaii 96779
Phone: 808-579-8320

Patients Without Time (Oahu)
P.O. Box 901
Haleiwa, Hawaii 96712
Phone: 808-284-2301
www.patientswithouttime.com

The Hemp & Cannabis Foundation Medical Clinic
Office Alliance Bldg, Suite 900
345 Queen St.
Honolulu, Hawaii 96813
Toll Free: 1-800-723-0188

www.thc-foundation.org/

Maine

Mainers for Medical Rights
www.mainers.org/act.htm

Montana

Montana Dept. Public Health & Human Services
Licensure Bureau
2401 Colonial Drive, P.O. Box 202953
Helena, Montana, 59620-2953.
Phone: 406-444-2676

Nevada

Nevada Dept. of Agriculture
P.O. Box 948
Carson City, Nevada 89707-0948
Phone: 775-684-5333 or 775-668-1180

Medical Marijuana Consultants of Nevada
1982 N. Rainbow Blvd. PMB #146
Las Vegas, Nevada 89108
Phone: 702-889-6626 (MMCN)
Email: Consultants@medicalmarijuananv.com
www.medicalmarijuananv.com

Medical Marijuana Referrals
Phone: 702-328-4420 (Las Vegas)
www.medicalmarijuanareferrals.com

Oregon

Oregon Dept. of Human Services
800 NE Oregon St.
Portland, Oregon 97232
Phone: 503-731-4002 Ext. 233, Fax: 503-872-6822
Email: OMMP.QA@state.or.us
http://egov.oregon.gov/DHS/ph/ommp/index.shtml

Alternative Medicine Outreach Program
455 W. Corey Ct.
Roseburg, Oregon 97470
Phone: 541-440-1934, Fax: 541-440-1943
www.amop.org

Compassion Center
2055 West 12th Ave.
Eugene, Oregon 97402
Phone: 541-484-6558, Fax: 541-484-0891
Email: email@compassioncenter.net
www.compassioncenter.net

MAMA
5217 SE 28th Ave.
Portland, Oregon 97202
Phone: 503-233-4202
Email: clinic@mamas.org
www.mamas.org

MERCY
1675 Fairgrounds Rd
Salem, Oregon 97303
Phone: 503-363-4588
Email: MERCY_Salem@hotmail.com
www.MercyCenters.org

Oregon NORML
Phone: 503-239-6110
www.ornorml.org

Stormy Ray Cardholders' Foundation
P.O. Box 220086
Portland, Oregon 97269
www.stormyray.org

The Hemp & Cannabis Foundation Medical Clinic
105 SE 18th Ave.
Portland, Oregon 97214
Phone: 503-281-5100, Toll Free: 1-800-723-0188
www.thc-foundation.org/

Voter Power
1505 SE Gideon Street
Suite #100
Portland, Oregon 97202
Phone: 503-224-3051, 503-235-5305, Fax:503-235-5365
www.voterpower.org

Rhode Island
The Division of Health Services Regulation
Rhode Island Department of Health
3 Capitol Hill
Providence, Rhode Island 02908
Phone: 401-222-2231 , Fax: 401-222-6548
www.health.state.ri.us/

Vermont
Marijuana Registry
Department of Public Safety
103 South Main Street
Waterbury, Vermont 05671
Phone: 802-241-5115
www.dps.state.vt.us/cjs/marijuana.htm

Washington
Washington State Dept. of Health
1112 SE Quince St.
P.O. Box 47890
Olympia, Washington 98504-7890
Phone: 800-525-0127 or 360-236-4052
Attention: Glenda Moore www.doh.wa.gov

Cannabis Compassion Medical Co-Op
Longview, Washington
Phone: 360-270-1910, Fax: 360-414-8025

Cannabis MD
www.cannabismd.org/

The Green Cross Patient Cooperative
PO Box 47347
Seattle, Washington 98146
Phone: 206-762-0630 , Fax: 206-762-7537
Email: greencross@hemp.net
www.hemp.net/greencross/

The Hemp and Cannabis Foundation Medical Clinic
Phone: 206-878-1701 (Seattle), Toll Free: 1-800-723-0188
www.thc-foundation.org/clinic.html

National

Marijuana Policy Project (MPP)

P.O. Box 77492
Capital Hill
Washington, D.C. 20013
Phone: 202-462-5747
http://www.mpp.org

NORML

1600 K Street, NW, Suite 501
Washington, D.C. 20003
Phone: 202-483-5500
http://www.norml.org

Model Medical Marijuana Bill

The Marijuana Policy Project's model medical marijuana legislation can be used in efforts to lobby state legislatures. The model bill is based on laws that have been passed by voters in eight states and by the Hawaii, Rhode Island and Vermont legislatures. It incorporates the lessons learned about the laws by patients, their advocates, physicians, lawyers, and government studies of those laws—including reports by the Vermont Medical Marijuana Study Commission and the U.S. General Accounting Office.

Because 99 percent of all marijuana arrests are made by state and local—not federal—officials, this bill can effectively protect 99 out of every 100 medical marijuana users who would otherwise face prosecution at the state level.

Be it enacted by the people of the state of _____:

Section 1. Title.

Sections 1 through 12 of this act shall be known as the _____ Medical Marijuana Act.

Section 2. Findings.

(a) Modern medical research has discovered beneficial uses for marijuana in treating or alleviating the pain, nausea, and other symptoms associated with certain debilitating medical conditions, as found by the National Academy of Sciences' Institute of Medicine in March 1999.

(b) According to the U.S. Sentencing Commission and the Federal Bureau of Investigation, 99 out of every 100 marijuana arrests in the U.S. are made under state law, rather than under federal law. Consequently, changing state law will have the practical effect of protecting from arrest the vast majority of seriously ill people who have a medical need to use marijuana.

(c) Although federal law currently prohibits any use of marijuana, the laws of Alaska, California, Colorado, Hawaii, Maine, Montana, Nevada, Oregon, Vermont, Rhode Island, and Washington permit the medical use and cultivation of marijuana. _____ joins in this effort for the health and welfare of its citizens.

(d) States are not required to enforce federal law or prosecute people for engaging in activities prohibited by federal law. Therefore, compliance with this act does not put the state of _____ in violation of federal law.

(e) State law should make a distinction between the medical and non-medical use of marijuana. Hence, the purpose of this act is to protect patients with debilitating medical conditions, and their practitioners and primary caregivers, from arrest and prosecution, criminal and other penalties, and property forfeiture if such patients engage in the medical use of marijuana.

(f) The people of the state of _____ declare that they enact this act pursuant to the police power to protect the health of its citizens that is reserved to the state of _____ and its people under the 10th Amendment to the United States Constitution.

Section 3. Definitions.

The following terms, as used in this act, shall have the meanings set forth in this section:

(a) "Debilitating medical condition" means:

(1) cancer, glaucoma, positive status for human immunodeficiency virus, acquired immune deficiency syndrome, Hepatitis C, or the treatment of these conditions;

(2) a chronic or debilitating disease or medical condition or its treatment that produces one or more of the following: cachexia or wasting syndrome; severe or chronic pain; severe nausea; seizures, including but not limited to those characteristic of epilepsy; or severe and persistent muscle spasms, including but not limited to those characteristic of multiple sclerosis and Crohn's disease; agitation of Alzheimer's disease; or

(3) any other medical condition or its treatment approved by the department, as provided for in section 5(a).

(b) "Department" means the _____ Department of Health or its successor agency.

(c) "Marijuana" has the meaning given that term in _____.

(d) "Medical use" means the acquisition, possession, cultivation, manufacture, use, delivery, transfer, or transportation of marijuana or paraphernalia relating to the consumption of marijuana to alleviate a registered qualifying patient's debilitating medical condition or symptoms associated with the medical condition.

(e) "Practitioner" means a person who is licensed with authority to prescribe drugs under section _____.

(f) "Primary caregiver" means a person who is at least 18 years old and who has agreed to assist with a person's medical use of marijuana. A primary caregiver may assist no more than five qualifying patients with their medical use of marijuana.

(g) "Qualifying patient" means a person who has been diagnosed by a practitioner as having a debilitating medical condition.

(h) "Registry identification card" means a document issued by the department that identifies a person as a qualifying patient or primary caregiver.

(i) "Usable marijuana" means the dried leaves and flowers of the marijuana plant, and any mixture or preparation thereof, but does not include the seeds, stalks, and roots of the plant.

(j) "Written certification" means a statement signed by a practitioner, stating that in the practitioner's professional opinion the potential benefits of the medical use of marijuana would likely outweigh the health risks for the qualifying patient. A written certification shall be made only in the course of a bona fide practitioner-patient relationship after the practitioner has completed a full assessment of the qualifying patient's medical history. The written certification shall specify the qualifying patient's debilitating medical condition or conditions.

Section 4. Protections for the Medical Use of Marijuana.

(a) A qualifying patient who has in his or her possession a registry identification card shall not be subject to arrest, prosecution, or penalty in any manner, or denied any right or privilege, including but not limited to civil penalty or disciplinary action by a business or occupational or professional licensing board or bureau, for the medical use of marijuana, provided that the qualifying patient possesses an amount of marijuana that does not exceed 12 marijuana plants and two-and-one-half ounces of usable marijuana.

(b) A primary caregiver who has in his or her possession a registry identification card shall not be subject to arrest, prosecution, or penalty in any manner, or denied any right or privilege, including but not limited to civil penalty or disciplinary action by a business or occupational or professional licensing board or bureau, for assisting a qualifying patient to whom he or she is connected through the department's registration process with the medical use of marijuana, provided that the primary caregiver possesses an amount of marijuana that does not exceed 12 marijuana plants and two-and-one-half ounces of usable marijuana for each qualifying patient to whom he or she is connected through the department's registration process.

(c) No school, employer, or landlord may refuse to enroll, employ, lease to, or otherwise penalize a person solely for his or her status as a registered qualifying patient or a registered primary caregiver.

(d) There shall exist a presumption that a qualifying patient or primary caregiver is engaged in the medical use of marijuana if the qualifying patient or primary caregiver:

(1) is in possession of a registry identification card; and

(2) is in possession of an amount of marijuana that does not exceed the amount permitted under this act. Such presumption may be rebutted by evidence that conduct related to marijuana was not for the purpose of alleviating the qualifying patient's debilitating medical condition or symptoms associated with the medical condition.

(e) A primary caregiver may receive reimbursement for costs associated with assisting with a registered qualifying patient's medical use of marijuana. Compensation shall not constitute sale of controlled substances.

(f) A practitioner shall not be subject to arrest, prosecution, or penalty in any manner, or denied any right or privilege, including but not limited to civil penalty or disciplinary action by the _____ Medical Board or by a another business or occupational or professional licensing board or bureau solely for providing written certifications or for otherwise stating that, in the practitioner's professional opinion, the potential benefits of the medical marijuana would likely outweigh the health risks for a patient.

(g)(1) Any interest in or right to property that is possessed, owned, or used in connection with the medical use of marijuana, or acts incidental to such use, shall not be forfeited.

(2) A law enforcement agency that seizes and does not return usable marijuana to a registered qualifying patient or a registered primary caregiver shall be liable to the cardholder for the fair market value of the marijuana.

(h) No person shall be subject to arrest or prosecution for constructive possession, conspiracy, aiding and abetting, being an accessory, or any other offense for simply being in the presence or vicinity of the medical use of marijuana as permitted under this act or for assisting a registered qualifying patient with using or administering marijuana.

(i) A registry identification card, or its equivalent, issued under the laws of another state, U.S. territory, or the District of Columbia to permit the medical use of marijuana by a qualifying patient, or to permit a person to assist with a qualifying patient's medical use of marijuana, shall have the same force and effect as a registry identification card issued by the department.

Section 5. Department to Issue Regulations.

(a) Not later than 90 days after the effective date of this act, the department shall promulgate regulations governing the manner in which it shall consider petitions from the public to add debilitating medical conditions to those included in this act. In considering such petitions, the department shall include public notice of, and an opportunity to comment in a public hearing upon, such petitions. The department shall, after hearing, approve or deny such petitions within 180 days of submission. The approval or denial of such a petition shall be considered a final department action, subject to judicial review. Jurisdiction and venue for judicial review are vested in the _____ Court. The denial of a petition shall not disqualify qualifying patients with that condition if they have a debilitating medical condition. The denial of a petition shall not prevent a person with the denied condition from raising an affirmative defense.

(b) Not later than 90 days after the effective date of this act, the department shall promulgate regulations governing the manner in which it shall consider applications for and renewals of registry identification cards for qualifying patients and primary caregivers. The department's regulations shall establish application and renewal fees that generate revenues sufficient to offset all expenses of implementing and administering this act. The department may vary the application and renewal fees along a sliding scale that accounts for a qualifying patient's income. The department may accept donations from private sources in order to reduce the application and renewal fees.

Section 6. Administering the Department's Regulations.

(a) The department shall issue registry identification cards to qualifying patients who submit the following, in accordance with the department's regulations:

(1) written certification;

(2) application or renewal fee;

(3) name, address, and date of birth of the qualifying patient, except that if the applicant is homeless, no address is required;

(4) name, address, and telephone number of the qualifying patient's practitioner; and

(5) name, address, and date of birth of each primary caregiver of qualifying patient, if any.

(b) The department shall not issue a registry identification card to a qualifying patient under the age of 18 unless:

(1) The qualifying patient's practitioner has explained the potential risks and benefits of the medical use of marijuana to the qualifying patient and to a parent, guardian, or person having legal custody of the qualifying patient; and

(2) A parent, guardian, or person having legal custody consents in writing to:

(A) allow the qualifying patient's medical use of marijuana;

(B) serve as one of the qualifying patient's primary caregivers; and

(C) control the acquisition of the marijuana, the dosage, and the frequency of the medical use of marijuana by the qualifying patient.

(c) The department shall verify the information contained in an application or renewal submitted pursuant to this section, and shall approve or deny an application or renewal within 15 days of receiving it. The department may deny an application or renewal only if the applicant did not provide the information required pursuant to this section, or if the department determines that the information provided was falsified. Rejection of an application or renewal is considered a final department action, subject to judicial review. Jurisdiction and venue for judicial review are vested in the _____ Court.

(d) The department shall issue a registry identification card to each primary caregiver, if any, who is named in a qualifying patient's approved application, up to a maximum of two primary caregivers per qualifying patient.

(e) The department shall issue registry identification cards within five days of approving an application or renewal, which shall expire one year after the date of issuance. Registry identification cards shall contain:

(1) name, address, and date of birth of the qualifying patient;

(2) name, address, and date of birth of each primary caregiver of qualifying patient, if any;

(3) the date of issuance and expiration date of the registry identification card;

(4) a random registry identification number; and

(5) a photograph, if the department decides to require one.

(f)(1) A qualifying patient who has been issued a registry identification card shall notify the department of any change in the qualifying patient's name, address, or primary caregiver, or if the qualifying patient ceases to have his or her debilitating medical condition, within 10 days of such change.

(2) A registered qualifying patient who fails to notify the department of any of these changes is responsible for a civil infraction, punishable by a fine of no more than $150. If the person has ceased to suffer from a debilitating medical condition, the card shall be deemed null and void, and the person shall be liable for any other penalties that may apply to the person's non-medical use of marijuana.

(3) A registered primary caregiver shall notify the department of any change in his or her name or address within 10 days of such change. A primary caregiver who fails to notify the department of any of these changes is responsible for a civil infraction, punishable by a fine of no more than $150.

(4) When a qualifying patient or primary caregiver notifies the department of any changes listed in this subsection, the department shall issue the registered qualifying patient and each primary caregiver a new registry identification card within 10 days of receiving the updated information and a $10 fee.

(5) When a qualifying patient who possesses a registry identification card changes his or her primary caregiver, the department shall notify the primary caregiver within 10 days. The primary caregiver's protections as provided in this act shall expire 10 days after notification by the department.

(6) If a registered qualifying patient or a primary caregiver loses his or her registry identification card, he or she shall notify the department and submit a $10 fee within 10 days of losing the card. Within five days, the department shall issue a new registry identification card with a new random identification number.

(g) Possession of, or application for, a registry identification card shall not constitute probable cause or reasonable suspicion, nor shall it be used to support the search of the person or property of the person possessing or applying for the registry identification card, or otherwise subject the person or property of the person to inspection by any governmental agency.

(h)(1) Applications and supporting information submitted by qualifying patients, including information regarding their primary caregivers and practitioners, are confidential.

(2) The department shall maintain a confidential list of the persons to whom the department has issued registry identification cards. Individual names and other identifying information on the list shall be confidential, exempt from the _____ Freedom of Information Act,

and not subject to disclosure, except to authorized employees of the department as necessary to perform official duties of the department.

(3) The department shall verify to law enforcement personnel whether a registry identification card is valid solely by confirming the random registry identification number.

(4) It shall be a crime, punishable by up to 180 days in jail and a $1,000 fine, for any person, including an employee or official of the department or another state agency or local government, to breach the confidentiality of information obtained pursuant to this act. Notwithstanding this provision, the department employees may notify law enforcement about falsified or fraudulent information submitted to the department.

(i) The department shall report annually to the legislature on the number of applications for registry identification cards, the number of qualifying patients and primary caregivers approved, the nature of the debilitating medical conditions of the qualifying patients, the number of registry identification cards revoked, and the number of practitioners providing written certification for qualifying patients. The department shall not provide any identifying information of qualifying patients, primary caregivers, or practitioners.

(j) Any state or local law enforcement official who knowingly cooperates with federal law enforcement agents to arrest, investigate, prosecute, or search a registered qualifying patient or a registered primary caregiver or his or her property for acting in compliance with this act shall have his or her employment suspended or terminated.

Section 7. Scope of Act.

(a) This act shall not permit:

(1) any person to undertake any task under the influence of marijuana, when doing so would constitute negligence or professional malpractice;

(2) the smoking of marijuana:

(A) in a school bus or other form of public transportation;

(B) on any school grounds;

(C) in any correctional facility; or

(D) in any public place; and

(3) any person to operate, navigate, or be in actual physical control of any motor vehicle, aircraft, or motorboat while under the influence of marijuana. However, a registered qualifying patient shall not be considered to be under the influence solely for having marijuana metabolites in his or her system.

(b) Nothing in this act shall be construed to require:

(1) a government medical assistance program or private health insurer to reimburse a person for costs associated with the medical use of marijuana; or

(2) an employer to accommodate the medical use of marijuana in any workplace.

(c) Fraudulent representation to a law enforcement official of any fact or circumstance relating to the medical use of marijuana to avoid arrest or prosecution shall be punishable by a fine of $500, which shall be in addition to any other penalties that may apply for making a false statement and for the non-medical use of marijuana.

Section 8. Affirmative Defense and Dismissal for Medical Marijuana.

(a)Except as provided in section 7, a person and a person's primary caregiver, if any, may assert the medical purpose for using marijuana as a defense to any prosecution involving marijuana, and such defense shall be presumed valid where the evidence shows that:

(1) a practitioner has stated that, in the practitioner's professional opinion, after having completed a full assessment of the person's medical history and current medical condition made in the course of a bona fide practitioner-patient relationship, the potential benefits of using marijuana for medical purposes would likely outweigh the health risks for the person; and

(2) the person and the person's primary caregiver, if any, were collectively in possession of a quantity of marijuana that was not more than was reasonably necessary to ensure the uninterrupted availability of marijuana for the purpose of alleviating the person's medical condition or symptoms associated with the medical condition.

(b) A person may assert the medical purpose for using marijuana in a motion to dismiss, and the charges shall be dismissed following an evidentiary hearing where the defendant shows the elements listed in Section 8(a).

(c) Any interest in or right to property that was possessed, owned, or used in connection with a person's use of marijuana for medical purposes shall not be forfeited if the person or the person's primary caregiver demonstrates the person's medical purpose for using marijuana pursuant to this section.

Section 9. Enforcment of this Act.

(a) If the department fails to adopt regulations to implement this act within 120 days of the effective date of this act, a qualifying patient may commence an action in a court of competent jurisdiction to compel the department to perform the actions mandated pursuant to the provisions of this act.

(b) If the department fails to issue a valid registry identification card in response to a valid application or renewal submitted pursuant to this act within 20 days of its submission, the registry identification card shall be deemed granted, and a copy of the registry identification application or renewal shall be deemed a valid registry identification card.

(c) If at any time after the 140 days following the effective date of this Act the department is not accepting applications, including if it has not created regulations allowing qualified patients to submit applications, a notarized statement by a qualified patient containing the information required in an application, pursuant to section 6 (a)(2-5), and a written certification shall be deemed a valid registry identification card.

Section 10. Repealer.

All laws and parts of laws in _____ that are in conflict with this act are hereby repealed.

Section 11. Severability.

Any section of this act being held invalid as to any person or circumstances shall not affect the application of any other section of this act that can be given full effect without the invalid section or application.

Section 12. Date of Effect.

This act shall take effect upon its approval.

Optional Section. Nonprofit Dispensaries.

(a) "Registered organization" means a nonprofit entity registered with the state under this act that acquires, possesses, cultivates, manufactures, delivers, transfers, transports, supplies, or dispenses marijuana, cultivation equipment, related supplies and educational materials, or marijuana seeds to registered qualifying patients and their primary caregivers. A registered organization is a primary caregiver, although it may supply marijuana to any number of registered qualifying patients who have designated it as one of their primary caregivers.

(b)(1) The department shall issue a registered organization license within 20 days to any person who complies with department rules and provides the following:

(A) a fee paid to the department in the amount established by the department, which shall not exceed $1,000;

(B) the name of the registered organization;

(C) the physical addresses of the registered organization and any other real property where marijuana is to be possessed, cultivated, manufactured, supplied, or dispensed relating to the operations of the registered organization; and

(D) the name, address, and date of birth of any person who is an agent of or employed by the registered organization.

(2) The department shall issue each agent and employee of a registered organization a registry identification card for a cost of $10 each within 10 days of receipt of the person's identifying information and the fee. Each card shall specify that the cardholder is an employee or agent of a registered organization.

(3) Each license for a registered organization and each employee or agent registry identification card shall expire one year after the date of issuance.

(4) Not later than 90 days after the effective date of this act, the department shall promulgate regulations to implement this section, including the following:

(A) procedures for the oversight of registered organizations, record-keeping and reporting requirements for registered organizations, the potential transference or sale of seized cultivation equipment and related supplies from law enforcement agencies to registered organizations, and procedures for suspending or terminating the registration of registered organizations; and

(B) the form and content of the registration and renewal applications.

(c) Registered organizations shall be subject to reasonable inspection by the department to determine that applicable rules are being followed. Reasonable notice shall be given prior to these inspections.

(d) (1) Registered organizations shall be established as nonprofit entities. They shall be subject to all applicable state laws governing nonprofit entities, but need not be recognized as a 501(c)(3) organization by the Internal Revenue Service;

(2) Registered organizations may not be located within 500 feet of the property line of a public school, private school, or structure used primarily for religious services or worship.

(3) The operating documents of a registered organization shall include procedures for the oversight of the registered organization and procedures to ensure adequate record-keeping.

(e)(1) A registered organization shall notify the department within 10 days of when an employee or agent ceases to work at the registered organization.

(2) The registered organization shall notify the department before a new agent or employee begins working at the registered organization, in writing, and it shall submit a $10 fee for that person's registry identification card.

(f)(1) No registered organization shall be subject to prosecution, search, seizure, or penalty in any manner, or denied any right or privilege, including but not limited to civil penalty or disciplinary action by a business or occupational or professional licensing board or bureau for acting in accordance with this act and the regulations issued pursuant thereto to assist registered qualifying patients to whom it is connected through the department's registration process with the medical use of marijuana, provided that the registered organization possesses an amount of marijuana which does not exceed 12 marijuana plants and two-and-one-half ounces of usable marijuana for each registered qualifying patient.

(2) No employees, agents, or board members of a registered organization shall be subject to arrest, prosecution, search, seizure, or penalty in any manner, or denied any right or privilege, including but not limited to civil penalty or disciplinary action by a

business or occupational or professional licensing board or bureau for working for a registered organization in accordance with this act.

(g) The registered organization is prohibited from:

(1) obtaining marijuana from outside the state in violation of federal law;

(2) acquiring, possessing, cultivating, manufacturing, delivering, transferring, transporting, supplying, or dispensing marijuana for any purpose except to assist registered qualifying patients with their medical use of marijuana directly or through the qualifying patients' other primary caregivers.

(h) Except as provided in this act, a municipality may not prevent a registered organization from operating in accordance with this act in an area where zoning permits retail businesses.

(i) If provisions of this act establishing registered organization are enjoined or declared unconstitutional, then enforcing laws against delivery of marijuana for consideration to registered qualifying patients shall be the lowest priority of law enforcement.

Cognitive Liberty

Picture this. The Tree of Knowledge under constant observation. Ceaseless, time-has-stopped, all-is-now scrutiny. Every approach watched by case-hardened wide-angle surveillance cameras. The mechanical whine of auto-focus motors and servomechanisms has replaced birdsong. Parabolic microphones wired into the branches, aimed at the ground below. Tripod-mounted close-up shots of each forbidden fruit. And all of this displayed in a central observation room. A room lit only by the light of high definition monitors showing picture after picture of bright red ripe fruits and The Tree from all perspectives. The genesis of suspicion and guilt. The theocracy of surveillance. All seeing, and always watching. Listening intently. Eat of the forbidden fruit and gain knowledge—but suffer God's wrath.

The genesis of the war on drugs is Genesis. The first prohibited substance was the fruit of the Tree of Knowledge; the first drug bust occurred in the Garden of Eden.

Long before Richard Nixon declared a "war on drugs," the stage was set, the props arranged and the players scripted. Everything follows, linearly, logically, in lockstep fashion to today. From the first two people arrested, convicted and punished for eating a forbidden fruit the US now arrests over 1.5 million people each

year for offenses involving forbidden drugs. More
people are arrested for drug offenses than for any other
category of crime. Their crime? Ingesting, providing, or
making, forbidden psychoactive plants, pills, powders,
and potions. Nature has been outlawed. Our own human
nature, our curiosity to "know," has been criminalized.

The seeds of authoritarian hostility toward the free
mind and body were planted in the fertile soils of the
Garden of Eden. And they have grown. The desire for
knowledge was tainted. Innate curiosity was recast as
evil temptation. Something deep inside us that yearns
to understand and to embody knowledge was forever
placed under the gaze of distrust.

This is the war on forbidden drugs, and much much
more. Question: Was the story of banishment from the
Garden, a story about a war on fruit? Is the war on
drugs really a war on drugs? Answer: No.

Some drugs, cannabis, mushrooms, poppies,
certain seeds and cacti, to name a few, have been
used for centuries as portals to an alternative type of
knowledge. The future holds more. The Garden is in
continual bloom, continual regeneration.

From the mythic time of our first ancestors, we have
lived under a near constant assault aimed at curiosity,
at knowing, at daring to explore oneself and one's
world, at claiming one's body and mind as one's own.
In the moment in which a person ingests a forbidden
fruit of knowledge, the body, mind, and spirit have
the potential to undergo a type of unification. The
blood-brain barrier grants entry, refusing to follow
governmental edicts. An alchemical transformation
occurs.

Adam and Eve were not given a chance. They were
not given the benefit of the doubt. They were not
permitted the freedom to show that they were capable

of handling their newly acquired knowledge. Merely
eating the forbidden fruit was warrant for punishment.
A little knowledge can be a dangerous thing, but by
most accounts knowledge is beneficial. Knowledge can
be used for good and for evil, to create and to destroy,
to free or to enslave. As the Sufis say, "All things have
two handles."

Under today's prohibition laws, merely possessing
a forbidden drug is grounds for arrest, criminal
conviction, and punishment. You need merely pick the
fruit. Yet, just as most people who use prescription
medicines use them responsibly, most people who
use forbidden drugs use them responsibly; they derive
the benefits elicited by the drug without causing any
harm to others. The crime exists only on paper, as
an edict, an authoritarian command barked from the
watchtower. There is only one narrative in the war on
drugs.

Distrust is the drug war's default value, along
with zero tolerance. We are treated like children,
infantilized, and instructed under threat of
imprisonment that aspects of our own consciousness
are off-limits. There is a Berlin Wall built within our
brains. Like Adam and Eve, we are banished from our
insides, prohibited and perpetually policed for fear that
we might ingest something that could radically change
how or what we think. Heaven forbid.

Visionary drugs can change our thinking as much
as books, and they are feared for the same reason.
The printing press, initially supported by the
ChurchState, first gave rise to the double-plus-good
mass-produced Bible. But it was then quickly used to
produce double-plus-bad documents of insurrection,
including "witchcraft" manuals. The quick result was a
crackdown, the issuing of rights to copy (copyright),
the banning and burning of certain books (the Index

Librorum Prohibitorum, was not abandoned until
1966). But was this a "war on books?" Was this a war
on paper and ink? No, it was a war on the ideas that
books carried, and in the same way the "war on drugs"
is a misnomer. It is a war on the shape and form and
content of consciousness.

In the Garden of Eden, God was positioned outside
of Adam and Eve, indeed, outside of all the plants and
animals in the Garden. Up above, removed, beyond.
Eating of the forbidden fruit turned Adam and Eve
inside. Understanding became directly available to
them, something that was found within rather than
without. After eating of the fruit they could make up
their own minds, reach their own conclusions, decide
for themselves. For this they were banished from the
Garden.

The Garden of Eden story did not banish only Adam
and Eve, it condemned esoteric knowledge. The quest
to go inside, to discover the secrets we all contain, to
find God within ourselves, was called to an immediate
halt. For the God presiding over the Garden, true
knowledge was caged outside of humans, divided apart
from them, available only by prior appointment. To
know the truth we are expected to travel a one-way
road leading outside of our despoiled selves to the
clean and tidy pages of the Bible whereupon all our
questions have been provided with answers. To seek
knowledge from within is cast as akin to searching for
light in a black hole.

In many respects, we remain no better off than
Adam and Eve. The federal government will not even
acknowledge that the cannabis plant can help to ease
the pain of some people suffering from chronic illness
for whom other medicines have failed. Peaceful people
as thin as skeletons have had their doors kicked in and
have been taken to jail for treating themselves with
forbidden drugs like marijuana.

Yet freedom has slowly, but steadily, marched forward: civil rights, women's rights, gay and lesbian rights, have all progressed despite monumental opposition by the authorities. The Berlin Wall did eventually come down. We are now at a point in history where the fight for bodily freedom must be joined by a complementary right to freedom of thought. To ignore freedom of thought is to sell freedom short and to draw arbitrary lines that excise explicit protections for the very aspect of ourselves that is most fundamental to who we are as human beings. We are now at a point in history where privacy, autonomy, and choice must be mapped beyond the body, so that they encompass and protect another dimension of what it means to be a free person. The civil liberty of the future is cognitive liberty. History shows that freedom does evolve, by both punctuated equilibrium and by the creative design of people who stand up and claim it.

Let's begin again. A future without freedom of thought is no future at all.

Advice for Marijuana Providers

by Dale Gieringer, Ph.D.

Despite the fact that scores of medical cannabis dispensaries, clubs, and delivery services are currently in business in California, the sale of medical cannabis is strictly illegal under federal law. Under state law, sale is generally illegal. However, non-profit "distribution" may be allowed in certain cases for patient cultivation co-ops and small-scale caregiver gardeners.

Under federal law, sale, cultivation and possession of marijuana remain strictly illegal. The DEA has raided dozens of medical marijuana growers, clubs and caregivers in California since the enactment of Prop. 215. For the most part, the targets have been either high-profile activists who have attracted publicity, or commercial-scale growers whom local law enforcement have decided to turn over for federal prosecution.

Under state law, the California Compassionate Use Act of 1996 (Prop. 215) exempts patients and their primary caregivers from criminal prosecution for personal possession and cultivation of marijuana, but *not* for distribution or sale to others.

California State law was expanded in 2004 by a
new law, SB 420 (Health & Safety Code 11362.7-8),
which (1) authorizes caregivers who provide marijuana
to patients to be compensated for the costs of their
services, though not on a for-profit
basis; and (2) allows patients *Dispensaries*
to form cultivation "collectives" *selling marijuana*
or "cooperatives." On careful *over the counter*
examination, however, neither *do so at the*
of these provisions provides a *tolerance of local*
green light for sales of cannabis. *authorities.*
Those dispensaries that are selling
marijuana over the counter accordingly do so at the
tolerance of local authorities. Note that there have
been instances where hostile local law enforcement
agencies have busted medical cannabis dispensaries
and charged their personnel with illegal distribution or
sales.

Caregivers

A "primary caregiver" is narrowly defined
under Prop. 215 to be "the individual designated
[by a legal patient] who has consistently assumed
responsibility for the housing, health, or safety of that
person." The law does not explicitly allow for multiple
caregivers. While caregivers may serve more than one
patient, a new provision in SB 420 has made it illegal
for them to have more than one patient outside their
own "city or county." While the constitutionality of
this provision is debatable because not only does it
seem to override Prop. 215, but the restriction to a
single "city or county" is ambiguous, so prospective
caregivers should beware of trying to serve large
geographical areas.

In general, the courts have held that cannabis clubs
cannot serve as legal "primary caregivers" for large
numbers of patients. Some persons have claimed

caregiver status while growing for multiple numbers
of patients on the theory that they are providing
for their patients' health or safety. This defense has
been successful in court for caregivers growing for
small numbers of patients. However, it was explicitly
rejected by a California state court of appeals in the
Peron decision, where the court held that Peron's San
Francisco Cannabis Buyers' Club could not reasonably
claim to function as a "primary caregiver" for its 8000
clients.

In general, medical cannabis providers who cater to
walk-in clients should not hope to rely on the caregiver
provision. Caregiver growers should limit themselves
to a select membership list of local clients whom they
personally know and who do not have other caregivers.
Within these constraints, SB 420 allows caregivers
to be compensated for the costs of their services,
but does NOT specifically authorize distribution or
cultivation for profit.

Collective Gardens

SB 420 encourages access to medical marijuana
through "collective, cooperative cultivation projects. "
Unfortunately, it provides no guidelines or explanation
as to how these should operate. Presumably, the basic
model is a group of patients and caregivers who plant a
garden together and share the crop among themselves.

The cultivation cooperative model does not necessarily
envision walk-in clients, nor retail sales of medicine to
members. Co-ops may be supported by participation
in work, donations or membership fees. Under one
model, co-op patients pay a set gardening fee for a
certain part of the crop, and receive the harvest at no
further charge. Unlike caregivers, collective gardens
aren't limited to patients from the same "city or
county."

A notable example of a patients' collective is the Wo/Men's Alliance for Medical Marijuana in Santa Cruz. WAMM has over 200 seriously ill members who cultivate a collective garden and attend to each others' health and personal needs. In 2004, WAMM won a federal injunction protecting their right to cultivate under the Raich decision. This did not stop the DEA from busting another collective garden , Eddy's Medicinal Gardens, whose operator was engaged in large-scale cultivation (30,000 plants) for some 2,000 ≠ 3,000 patients. The WAMM injunction was voided in 2005 by the Supreme Court's Raich decision.

Two examples of patients' providers officially structured as "cooperative" corporations under California law were the Oakland Cannabis Buyers' Cooperative and Los Angeles Cannabis Research Center. Both would have been legal under SB 420, but both were shut down by the federal government.

The legality of collectives and cooperatives was upheld by the California Third District Court of Appeals in the 2005 Urziceanu decision. The Court ruled that while Prop. 215 did not authorize distribution by anyone except primary caregivers, SB 420 allowed for distribution among patients and caregivers through collectives and cooperatives.

Federal Law

Under the U.S. Controlled Substances Act (CSA), marijuana is currently classified as a Schedule I drug, meaning that it has no accepted medical use. The federal government has interpreted the law strictly to mean that all marijuana is illegal regardless of state laws like Prop. 215. The federal law was upheld by the U.S. Supreme Court in the case Raich v Gonzalez (2005), where it ruled that the CSA's ban on posssession and cultivation did not exceed the federal government's constitutional authority under the interstate commerce clause even in the case of private, personal use by patients. While further constitutional challenges to the CSA are being pursued in federal court, medical marijuana remains completely illegal under current federal law.

The Supreme Court rejected a prior 2001 challenge to the federal law by upholding an injunction ordering the Oakland Cannabis Buyers Cooperative and five other cannabis clubs to cease operations. The court overturned a Ninth Circuit Court of Appeals ruling that the OCBC was entitled to a "medical necessity" defense for distributing marijuana to its members. While the court ruled for the government on the procedural grounds that the CSA did not allow for a necessity defense for distributors, it left open the question whether individual patients might invoke a necessity defense.

Federal Forfeiture

Another federal weapon against medical marijuana is property forfeiture. Federal law allows the government to forfeit real estate from owners or landlords who let it be used for marijuana distribution or cultivation. The DEA successfully used forfeiture against the Los Angeles Cannabis Resource Center in 2001. The LACRC's building was actually owned by the city of West Hollywood, which had bought it as a gift for the club. The government had no trouble taking possession of it by means of forfeiture, effectively closing the LACRC.

More recently, the government invoked forfeiture to close the Capitol Compassionate Care Center in Roseville and to force a landlord to evict another dispensary in West Hollywood. The DEA has threatened to employ forfeiture more widely. So far, the chosen targets have mostly been facilities that actively sought publicity through the media or advertising. Dispensary operators are advised to operate discreetly to avoid DEA attention.

Local Regulation

Despite the shaky legality of California dispensaries, many cities and counties have enacted ordinances aimed at zoning, regulating, or limiting them. Some localities have enacted moratoriums banning new dispensaries altogether, including numerous towns in the Central Valley area and the Peninsula. Others, including Alameda County, Hayward, Berkeley, Santa Rosa, West Hollywood, and Oakland, have put a limit on the number of dispensaries in their area.

A few cities, including San Francisco, Oakland, West Hollywood, and Santa Rosa have established licensing schemes for dispensaries. Strict zoning regulations are in effect in many localities. Other regulations that have been adopted include banning on-site consumption and limiting the quantity of marijuana that can be sold or kept on hand.

Openning a Dispensary

Anyone interested in opening a medical cannabis facility should be wary about alarming local authorities. Many towns have moved to ban dispensaries after receiving inquiries from prospective operators. However, anyone planning to open a storefront dispensary should seek a business license and comply with local zoning regulations. It is especially important that dispensaries be appropriately sited so as not to disturb neighbors. Neighborhood

Dispensary should seek a business license, comply with local zoning regulations, and be proactive in getting along with neighbors..

complaints are the number one cause of police raids.
Dispensaries should also be sure that their landlords
are comfortable with what they are doing. Landlord
complaints are another leading cause of problems.

Dispensaries have been organized in various ways:
as sole proprietorships, partnerships, non-profit
cooperatives or corporations. Because SB 420 does not
specifically protect for-profit operations, non-profit
organizations are probably safer. Prospective operators
are advised to consult a business attorney.

Sales Tax

The California State Board of Equalization
has ruled that medical cannabis sales are subject to
sales tax, regardless of their legality. This is consistent
with California law, under which medicinal herbs are
generally taxable. The only medicines that are not
taxable are those provided in licensed pharmacies with
a physician's prescription.

Attorneys

Prospective patient providers are strongly
advised to consult an attorney. The following attorneys
are familiar with the law on cannabis cooperatives,
patients' groups, dispensaries, etc.

—Dale Gieringer
State Coordinator
California NORML

Bibliography

Bearman v. Superior Court, 117 Cal.App.4th 463, (2004).

Bonnie & Whitebread. *The Marijuana Conviction.* New York, NY: The Lindesmith Center. (1999)

Booth, Martin. *Cannabis: A History.* New York, NY: St. Martin's Press. (2003)

Christie, T. Marijuana Doctor Gets Probation, $5,000 Fine. *The Register Guard.* (2002, April 13)

Commonwealth v. Hutchins, 575 N.E.2d 741 (Mass. 1991).

Conant v. Walters, 309 F.3d 629, (9th Cir. 2002).

Conrad, C. *Hemp for Health.* Rochester, VT: Healing Arts Press. (1997)

Drug Enforcement Administration. *In the Matter of Marijuana Rescheduling Petition* (Docket No. 86-22). (1988)

Gardner, F. Marijuana Specialist Defends his Practice. *The Berkeley Daily Planet.* (2003A, May 2)

Gardner, F. Mikuriya's Motion Denied. *Anderson Valley Advertiser.* (2003B, Aug. 6)

Gardner, F. Is the Medical Board on a Crusade? *Anderson Valley Advertiser.* (2003C, May 21)

Gardner, F. Dr. Leveque's License Revoked. *Anderson Valley Advertiser.* (2004, Oct. 27).

Gordon, T. Judge Says Drug Wasn't A Medical Necessity. *The Daily Herald.* (2003, June 10).

Gonzales v. Raich, 125 S.Ct. 2195, 2201, Slip Op. 03-1454 (2005).

Idaho v. Hastings, 801 P.2d 563 (Idaho 1990).

Jeffries, D. & Jeffries, L *Jeffrey's journey.* Oakland, CA: Quick American Publishing Company. (2005).

Jenks v. Florida, 582 So.2d 676 (Ct.App. 1st Dist., FL. 1991). See also, Sowell v. Florida, 738 So.2d 333 (Ct. App. 1st Dist., FL. 1998).

Maddaus, G. Claim Nets Cash for Confiscated Stash. *Los Angeles Times.* (2001, Nov. 28).

McMahon & Largen, *Prescription pot.* Far Hills, NJ: New Horizon Press. (2003).

Minnesota v. Hanson, 468 N.W.2d 77 (Minn. Ct. App. 1991).

National Commission on Marihuana, *Marihuana: A Signal of Misunderstanding.* (1972).

New Jersey v. Tate, 505 A.2d 941 (N.J. 1986).

Oregon v. Kama, 39 P.3d 866 (Or. App. 2002).

People ex rel. Lungren v. Peron, 59 Cal. App. 4th 1383 (1997).

People v. Galambos, 104 Cal.App.4th 1147 (Cal.App. 2002)

Randall & O'Leary. *Marijuana Rx: The Patients' Fight for Medicinal Pot.* New York, NY: Thunder's Mouth Press. (1998).

Rosenfeld, S. Insurer Pays Client on Pot Seizure. *San Francisco Examiner.* (1999, Sept. 7).

Rosenthal, Mikuriya, & Gieringer. *Marijuana Medical Handbook: A Guide to Therapeutic Use.* Oakland, CA: Quick American Publishing Company. (1997)

Ross v. Ragingwire Telecommunications, 132 Cal.App.4th 590 (2005).

Sanchez, E. Insuring Medical Marijuana: Some Policyholders with Prescriptions Cash in After Pot Taken. *Sacramento Bee.* (2000, June 12).

San Francisco Board of Supervisors *Resolution 141-92.* (1992).

United States v. Bailey, 444 U.S. 394, 415-16 (1980).

United States v. Burton, 894 F.2d 188 (6th Cir. 1990).

United States v. Oakland Cannabis Buyers' Cooperative, 532 U.S. 483 (2001).

United States v. Randall, 104 Daily Wash.L. Rep. 2249 (Super.Ct.D.C. Nov. 24, 1976).

Washburn v. Columbia Forest Products, Inc., CC 0012-12516; SC S52254 (Or. 2006).

Washington v. Butler, 126 Wn. App. 741, 109 P.3d 493 (Wash.Ct.App. 2005).

Washington v. Shepherd, 110 Wn. App. 544, 41 P.3d 1235 (Wash. Ct. App. 2002) review denied, 147 Wn. 2d 1017, 56 P.3d 992 (Wash. 2002).

Wickard v. Filburn, 317 U.S. 111 (1942).

Wilson, T. States Medicinal Pot Law Proves to be Can of Worms. *Los Angeles Times.* (2003, July 23).

Zimmer & Morgan, *Marijuana Myths, Marijuana Facts.* New York, NY: The Lindesmith Center. (1997).

Index

THE **L**AW **F**IRM OF **R**ICHARD **G**LEN **B**OIRE focuses exclusively on appeals, expungements, and other post-conviction legal relief in criminal cases. Mr. Boire is a leading legal authority on marijuana, ecstasy, khat, research chemicals, and psychedelics (a.k.a., entheogens, visionary substances, hallucinogens, analogues, and/or shamanic inebriants).

Mr. Boire received his law degree in 1990 from UC Berkeley's School of Law (Boalt Hall), one of the best law schools in the country.

He testified about Ecstasy before the United States Sentencing Commission in Washington, DC, and before the California Public Safety Committee. In each case, his testimony helped produce lower penalties for ecstasy than those under consideration.

In addition to his private law practice, he served as legal counsel for the Center for Cognitive Liberty & Ethics, a law and policy center devoted to protecting freedom of thought and the unlimited potential of the human mind.

Mr. Boire is a member of the California Bar and has been admitted to practice before the Ninth Circuit Court of Appeals, as well as the United States Supreme Court. He is a member of the National Association of Criminal Defense Attorney's, the NORML Legal Committee, the American Bar Association, and the California Bar Association.

You will not find an attorney more skilled or more dedicated to doing everything possible to resolve your criminal case in your favor. We are happy to be of service.

www.convictionfree.com

Kevin Feeney, an Oregon based attorney, published the *Oregon Medical Marijuana Law Reporter*, a tri-annual law journal that tracks and examines changes and advances in marijuana law, both nationally and at the state level. Mr. Feeney works in the field of drug and alcohol treatment, and serves on the Board of Directors for the Compassion Center, a non-profit organization serving medical marijuana patients in the state of Oregon.

lalunaensumano@hotmail.com

About the Marijuana Policy Project

With more than 20,000 dues-paying members and more than 100,000 e-mail subscribers, the Marijuana Policy Project is the largest marijuana policy reform organization in the United States. Incorporated as a nonprofit organization in 1995, MPP works to minimize the harm associated with marijuana — both the consumption of marijuana and the laws that are intended to prohibit such use.

MPP believes that the greatest harm associated with marijuana is prison. To this end, MPP focuses on removing criminal penalties for marijuana use, with a particular emphasis on making marijuana medically available to seriously ill people who have the approval of their doctors.

MPP's Vision Statement

MPP envisions a country with public policies that allow for the responsible medical and non-medical use of marijuana, and minimize the harms associated with marijuana consumption and the laws that manage its use.

MPP's Mission Statement

MPP pursues its work along two parallel tracks — making marijuana medically available to patients in need (known as "legalizing medical marijuana"), and taxing and regulating marijuana for general adult use (known as "marijuana regulation"). Specifically, MPP pursues the following mission (strategies) to achieve its vision:

1. Increase public support for marijuana regulation.
2. Identify and activate supporters of medical marijuana and marijuana regulation.
3. Change state laws to legalize medical marijuana and/or regulate marijuana.
4. Increase the credibility of marijuana policy reform on Capitol Hill.

www.mpp.org

Frank H. Lucido,MD graduated from University of Michigan Medical School and completed his Family Practice Residency through University of California at Davis. He practices Family and General Medicine in Berkeley, California. Since the passage of the California Compassionate Use Act of 1996, Dr. Lucido has been performing Medical Cannabis evaluations, and writes and lectures on the subject. Dr. Lucido is a member of Society of Cannabis Clinicians, and Physicians for Social Responsibility. He co-authored the widely read article "Implementation of the Compassionate Use Act in a Family Medical Practice, Seven Years' Clinical Experience" with Mariavittoria Mangini, PhD, FNP, published the *Journal of the Society of Cannabis Clinicians,* which is a blueprint for physicians in making safe and appropriate recommendations. Dr, Lucido founded MedicalBoardWatch.com to keep watch on Medical Board of California actions against physicians who make medical cannabis recommendations. Dr. Lucido also founded Lucido Medical-Legal Consulting to give expert medical testimony for legitimate patients who use cannabis medicinally, and for responsible physicians who recommend it appropriately. He lectures on medical cannabis, and practice standards, and is interested in speaking to physician groups to increase the number of responsible physicians willing to make appropriate recommendations for this safe and effective medicine.

DrFrank@DrLucido.com   510-848-0958

www.DrLucido.com   www.MedicalBoardWatch.com

Dale Gieringer, PhD is the state coordinator of California NORML, and a co-founder of the California Drug Policy Reform Coalition and of Californians for Compassionate Use and one of the organizers and co-authors of California's medical marijuana initiative, Proposition 215. Dr. Gieringer received his Ph.D. from Stanford on the topic of DEA drug regulation. He is the author of articles on marijuana and driving safety, drug testing, marijuana health mythology, the economics of marijuana legalization, and DEA "drug enforcement abuse." He has sponsored research on the use of water pipes and vaporizers to reduce harmful tars in marijuana smoke.

dpfca@igc.org

Just say NORML!

C alifornia **NORML** is a non-profit, membership
organization dedicated to reforming California's
marijuana laws. Our mission is to establish the right
of adults to use cannabis legally. We are the only state
organization devoted specifically to marijuana reform.
We publish a newsletter, lobby lawmakers, sponsor
events, offer legal, educational, and consumer health
advice, and sponsor scientific research. We maintain a
separate membership and financial base from national
NORML.

California NORML was originally founded as Amorphia, which
organized the 1972 California Marijuana Initiative, Prop. 19.
The initiative, which would have repealed laws against adult
use, possession and cultivation of marijuana, received 33%
of the vote. Amorphia became the California branch of the
National Organization for the Reform of Marijuana Laws in
1974.

California NORML successfully lobbied the state legislature
to pass the Moscone Act of 1975, which "decriminalized"
marijuana possession from a felony to a misdemeanor, with a
maximum $100 fine for 1 ounce or less.

California NORML attorneys successfully sued to force CAMP
(Campaign Against Marijuana Planting) helicopters to respect
a 500' flying ceiling.

California NORML led the opposition to Gov. Wilson's "Smoke
a Joint, Lose Your License" law, imposing a six-month driver's
license suspension for pot possession, which was killed as of
July, 1, 1999.

California NORML was one of the original sponsors of the
Compassionate Use Act of 1996, Proposition 215, the nation's
first medical marijuana law.

Through the Medical Marijuana Patients' and Caregivers' Fund
and the NORML Foundation, California NORML has supported
the legal battle to uphold Prop. 215 against federal intrusion.

www.canorml.org